SPICY
TEX-MEX COOKING

© Naumann & Göbel Verlagsgesellschaft mbH, a subsidiary of
VEMAG Verlags- und Medien Aktiengesellschaft, Cologne
www.apollo-intermedia.de

Complete production: Naumann & Göbel Verlagsgesellschaft mbH, Cologne
Printed in Italy

ISBN 3-625-11091-1

SPICY
TEX-MEX COOKING

CONTENTS

INTRODUCTION

Tex-Mex cooking, its origins
and special ingredients:
here you will find everything
you need to know.

What is Tex-Mex cooking?

Tex-Mex cooking is not just a colourful, interesting and fascinating art of cooking, it is also a Weltanschauung, a way of perceiving the world: a live multicultural phenomenon that effortlessly keeps integrating new elements.

This style of cooking was developed in the Southwest of the USA – in Texas, Arizona and New Mexico. It is an expressive mixture of mostly Mexican but also Indian, Spanish and other European elements.

However, it is not possible to track down today which of these cultures has had the biggest influence on eating habits. The fact remains that many Indian foodstuffs such as maize, tomatoes, beans, melons and chillies were cultivated by the European conquerors and settlers and were integrated into their cooking.

Tex-Mex cooking is open for new creations and even today breathes the smell of freedom and adventure – be it during traditional cooking of chilli out in the open or during a hearty barbecue with baked pota-toes, steaks, spareribs, grilled corn on the cob and lots of chilled beer.

The soul of Tex-Mex cooking lies in tortillas, chillies, beans and cheese. Many aficionados have taken these ingredients and the local vegetables and fruits and have over the course of centuries developed a colourful and multifaceted cooking that is unique in the entire world.

Chillies

The slim relatives of the bell peppers can be devilishly pungent or mild to fruity-sweet. In Tex-Mex cooking, there is a wide choice of varieties. It is even said that there is a special kind of chilli for every day of the year.

More than 5000 years ago, Native Americans discovered the savoury, tiny berry fruits growing wild. They used them to marinate their chunks of meat, which until then had been rather tasteless.

European conquerors and explorers were responsible for spreading the chilli plant to Africa, Asia and Europe. "Cooky", the cook and as such the most important person on the big cattle trails, introduced the chillies into the cooking of the Southwestern US. A good cook knew how to keep the tough cowboys in a good mood and so chilli plants were first cultivated along the trails.

This was simple, because the plants thrived on very little care. In the course of the years, the tiny berries developed into a multitude of varieties with different forms of fruit, ranging from longish and small to round to nearly square in form. What's more, chilli pods shine in the most wonderful colours: from light yellow to green, orange and red through to purple, brown and black. With a few exceptions, the small species are more pungent than the larger ones.

The fully grown fruit has a straight, smooth skin, is hollow inside with plenty of seeds and a fleshy core. If you cannot find fresh pods, buy them either dried, pickled or ground. Keep in mind that dried chilli can be much more pungent than fresh chilli, especially if it has not been seeded. Good, fresh chilli powder can be recognised by the somewhat coarse consistency and the deep red colour.

When handling chilli, you should be very careful. The agent Capsaicin does not only give the chilli its pungency, but also reacts on skin. If you are very sensitive, you might prefer wearing rubber gloves when handling chillies; never touch your eyes with your fingers and wash your hands thoroughly afterwards. Since most of the spice lies in the seeds and the core of the pods, chilli dishes can be made to taste milder if you remove seeds and core. If you prefer it a little more pungent, use the whole pod.

Sometimes, the skin of the chilli tastes bitter and it can be hard to digest. It can be peeled if you heat up the chillies in the oven or under the grill, until the skin starts to blister. However, the fruit's flesh should not burn during this process. Dried chillies can be stir-fried for a short while and then soaked in hot water for approximately 10 minutes. This way, they develop a very special aroma. Afterwards, carefully slit open the chilli pods and remove seeds and core.

Pull off the dark skin.

Cut out the core.

When shopping, choose firm, shiny pods with intact skin. Dried chillies should also be flawless and should still be a little elastic.

9

Maize

Maize is one of the most important staple foods in Tex-Mex cooking. Maize and beans complement each other in their biological value and are good providers of proteins. The Maya people evidently already knew about this when they began cultivating this plant over 5000 years ago. They attributed divine powers to the maize, because in their myth of creation, the gods fashioned the first man from white and yellow corn cobs.

The traditional Masa, the maize dough used for tortillas, is made of maize grains. The white grains are soaked in warm, chalky water, skinned and ground. Water and salt are added to make a paste that quickly goes bad. The dough should either be used immediately or frozen in portions.

Masa Harina is maize flour – you could call it a kind of dried Masa – and is turned into tortilla dough with water and oil. It is used as a substitute for fresh Masa, which is complicated to produce. It can be bought in specialist shops as "maize for ponzole".

Burritos: These are tortillas filled with meat.

Chilaquiles: This is nothing other than the tortilla leftovers, broken into pieces or cut into slices and fried in oil until crispy brown.

Enchiladas: This term is used for all tortillas served with chilli sauce.

Nachos: These are grilled tortilla chips. They can be cut from ready-made tortillas or prepared from fresh dough and then fried. Nachos are covered with various ingredients and then grilled with cheese. The most famous recipe is "Nachos with Chorizo". Chorizo is a savoury, air-dried sausage made of minced pork that you will be able to find in Spanish specialist shops. The best cheese to use is Cheddar.

Quesadillas: This term refers to all filled tortillas.

Tacos: These are tortillas formed into bowls that can be filled with ingredients. Ready-made taco shells can be found in every large supermarket.

Tamales: A soft pastry made of maize flour, pasted onto dried maize leaves and then steamed in them. Usually, the pastry is filled and there are manifold possibilities concerning the ingredients and tastes. Instead of maize leaves, you can also use greased tin foil or greaseproof paper.

Tortilla chips: Roll out fresh tortilla dough very thinly, cut it into triangles, add some ground paprika, chilli powder or pepper, and then fry them. It's a wonderful snack with beer or wine.

Tortillas: They are the bread in Tex-Mex cooking and often also serve as plate or as spoon. They are served as side dishes with nearly every dish and are used in numerous specialities. Maize tortillas are made of freshly prepared Masa or of a dough made of Masa Harina. There are also wheat flour tortillas, which, as the name already tells, are made of wheat flour. In Mexico and in the Southwestern States of the US, freshly made tortillas can be bought on as good as every street corner. We have to resort to specialist shops. Of course you can also prepare them yourself: in this book, you will find recipes for both maize and wheat flour tortillas.

Tostadas: This is the term for fried tortillas, that can also be used as edible plates.

Salsa and Mole

The Spanish term Salsa means nothing other than sauce, but not every sauce that is prepared for Tex-Mex cooking is a salsa. One typical trait of the salsa is that its ingredients are usually used raw. Any mixture of ingredients can be used for a salsa, but the most common ingredients are chillies, tomatoes, garlic and onions. Every housewife has her own special recipe that she swears by. In the chapter "Salads, Side Dishes, Sauces and Vegetables" you will find numerous recipes that will help you prepare your own, home-made salsa. In Tex-Mex cooking, salsas are usually served as a savoury accompaniment to meat dishes, with every guest serving him or herself as he or she pleases.

Ingredients should only be pureed if it says so in the recipe. It is usually better to finely chop everything and leave it with a little bite to it. A salsa tastes best when left to draw for about one hour. The "Salsa Endiablada" is world-famous and called devil's sauce because of its spiciness. It can be bought as a ready-made bottled product. Salsas turn out particularly savoury when tomatillos (green tomatoes) are used instead of the usual tomatoes. Like the tomatoes, they

belong to the family of Solanaceae, but they look like small limes. The slightly sour taste is also similar to that of limes.

Mole is the Indian term for a rich sauce or herb mixture containing chilli. Its special feature is that the mole has to be simmered over a low heat for a long time. Mole is usually served with meat; either the meat is cooked in the mole, or the mole is prepared by itself and served with grilled meat. There are endless

variations to these delicious sauces, ranging from mole soup, a vegetable stew of Spanish origin, to the Poblano mole, a dish served on festive occasions which is said to have been created in a Mexican monastery in the 17th century. The original recipe contains more than 100 ingredients, with bitter chocolate being an indispensable component. Poblano mole is traditionally served with turkey.

STARTERS AND SNACKS

Tortillas, burritos, tacos and tamales:
this chapter introduces you with
classics of Tex-Mex cooking that
also taste good as main courses.

BURRITOS FILLED WITH MINCED MEAT

Serves 4

450 g/1 lb wheat flour

1 tsp salt

1 tsp bicarbonate of soda

1 tbsp lard

180 ml/6 fl oz water

4 tbsp oil

1 onion

1 bunch spring onions

500 g/17 oz minced meat

Salt

Freshly ground pepper

2 tbsp butter

75 ml/2.5 fl oz beer

20 ml/scant 1 oz soy sauce

Chilli powder

Parsley to garnish

Preparation time: approx. 45 minutes

Nutrition information per serving approx.: 40 g P, 49 g F, 82 g C, 989 kcal/4156 kJ

1 Make a smooth dough out of the flour, salt, bicarbonate of soda, lard and water.

2 Form the dough into 12 small balls and roll them out into flat loaves of approx. 10 cm/4" Ø between two layers of tin foil.

3 Heat the oil in a frying pan and fry the flat loaves for several minutes from both sides. They are ready when the edges lift up slightly and they have taken on a light brown shade.

4 Cover and store them in a warm place. Peel and coarsely chop the onion. Peel and clean the spring onions, then cut them into rings.

5 Season the minced meat with salt and pepper. Heat the butter in a frying pan and gently fry the meat with the onion and spring onions. Add beer and soy sauce. Season to taste with chilli powder.

6 Spread the burritos out on the work table, spread the meat mixture on them, roll them up and garnish with parsley.

Make a smooth dough.

Form 12 balls.

Roll out into flat loaves.

Bake the loaves ...

... until they are slightly brown.

NACHOS TEXICANA WITH BELL PEPPER AND SWEET CORN

100 g/ 3.5 oz tortilla chips

200 g/7 oz turkey breast

Worcestershire sauce

1 tbsp sunflower oil

Salt

Pepper

1/2 red bell pepper

340 g/12 oz sweet corn (tinned)

50 ml/2 fl oz chilli sauce or salsa verde (ready-made)

120 g/4 oz grated cheddar

Preparation time: approx. 45 minutes

Nutrition information per serving approx.: 22 g P, 14 g F, 23 g C, 332 kcal/1395kJ

1 Spread the tortilla chips on a baking tray. Wash the meat, pat dry and cut into slices. Season with Worcestershire sauce.

2 Heat the oil in a frying pan and fry the meat. Season with salt and pepper. Pre-heat the oven to 220 °C/425 °F/gas mark 7.

3 Trim and rinse the bell pepper and cut into cubes. Stir sweet corn, bell pepper and salsa together and warm up a little.

4 Spread the meat and the cooled vegetable sauce over the tortillas and spread cheese on top.

5 Bake in the centre of the oven for 5–10 minutes.

MEXICAN ENCHILADAS JOSÉ

1 Mix the flour with the maize semolina, salt and egg. Slowly add 450 ml/16 fl oz of water and make into a thin pancake dough. Put aside for approx. 30 minutes.

2 Heat the oil in a frying pan, make 8 thin maize flat loaves of approx. 20 cm/8" Ø from the dough and bake them until they have turned a light yellow, then place them on top of each other.

3 Cut the ham into small cubes. Trim and rinse the spring onions and cut into rings. Mix the quark with the salsa and stir in the ham and spring onions.

4 Pre-heat the oven to 200 °C/390 °F/ gas mark 6. Put 2 tbsp of the quark mixture into the middle of the flat loaves and fold them up.

5 Place on a baking tray lined with greaseproof paper and bake in the centre of the oven for approx. 15 minutes. Garnish the enchiladas with herbs and serve.

■ **Serves 4**

100 g/3.5 oz flour

100 g/3.5 oz maize semolina

1/2 tsp salt

1 egg

1 tbsp sunflower oil

200 g/7 oz ham

2 spring onions

250 g/9 oz quark

5 tbsp chilli sauce (ready-made)

Herbs to garnish

Preparation time: approx. 40 minutes

Standing time: approx. 30 minutes

Nutrition information per serving approx.: 13 g P, 14 g F, 38 g C, 359 kcal/1507 kJ

MAIZE TORTILLAS WITH SPICY MEAT SAUCE

■ Serves 4

450 g/1 lb maize flour

1 tsp salt

4 tbsp oil

2 red chillies

80 g/2.75 oz goat's cream cheese

200 g/7 oz minced meat

Salt

Freshly ground pepper

Chilli powder

3 tbsp butter

50 g/2 fl oz taco sauce (ready-made in jars)

Parsley, chives and tomato slices for garnishing

Preparation time: approx. 45 minutes

Nutrition information per serving approx.: 19 g P, 29 g F, 78 g C, 702 kcal/2948 kJ

1 Pour maize flour, salt and approx. 300 ml/10 fl oz water into a large bowl and make into a smooth dough.

2 If the dough is sticky, it is too wet, then you should add some more flour.

3 Form the dough into 12 small balls and roll each ball out between two sheets of cling film into flat loaves of approx. 12 cm/4.5" Ø.

4 Heat the oil in a frying pan and fry the tortillas on both sides for several minutes. They are ready when the edges turn upwards and are slightly brown.

5 Rinse the chillies, cut in halves, remove the seeds and finely chop the pods.

6 In a bowl, mix the goat's cheese with the minced meat and the chopped chillies, season with salt, pepper and chilli powder.

7 Heat the butter in a frying pan and fry the meat. Stir in the taco sauce and season to taste with salt, pepper and chilli powder.

8 Arrange the meat sauce and tortillas on plates and garnish with parsley, chives and tomato slices.

MAIZE TORTILLAS

Home-made maize tortillas are especially tasty. Ready-made maize tortillas can be bought in shops specialising in American cooking.

MEXICO-BURGERS WITH SPINACH

■ **Serves 4**

1 tbsp sunflower seeds

1 onion

4 tbsp sunflower oil

150 g/5 oz frozen spinach

Salt

Freshly ground pepper

60 g/2 oz maize semolina

2 tbsp flour

1 egg

A few lettuce leaves

1 tomato

1/4 cucumber

1/2 red bell pepper

1/2 yellow bell pepper

4 rolls

2 tbsp chilli sauce (ready-made)

Preparation time: approx. 45 minutes

Nutrition information per serving approx.: 10 g P, 10 g F, 36 g C, 295 kcal/1242 kJ

1 Roast the sunflower seeds in a frying pan without using any fat. Peel and chop the onion.

2 Heat 2 tbsp oil in a frying pan and fry the onions. Add the spinach and steam. Season with salt and pepper.

3 Add 1/4 l/9 fl oz water. Stir in maize semolina, bring to the boil and leave to simmer over a low heat for approx. 10 minutes. Towards the end, stir in 2 tbsp flour, the egg and sunflower seeds.

4 Heat the remaining oil in a frying pan. With a spoon, divide the dough into 4 portions, place in the pan, even out a little and fry the burgers on both sides.

5 Trim and rinse lettuce, tomato, cucumber and bell pepper and cut into slices.

6 Cut the rolls, pasting some of the salsa on every half. Then garnish with lettuce, tomato, cucumber and bell pepper slices, and top with the spinach-maize semolina burgers.

Portion the dough.

Even out the burgers.

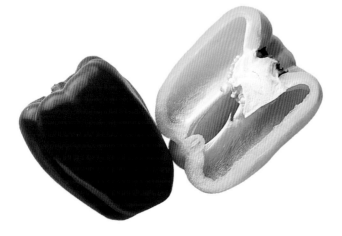

TACOS FILLED WITH TENDER CHICKEN

SUGGESTED DRINK

As matching aperitif to go with the tacos filled with chicken, we recommend tequila with a shot of lime and pineapple juice. Serve the drink garnished with an olive and a slice of lime.

■ Serves 4

150 g/5 oz flour

1 tsp salt

1/2 ripe avocado

Lemon juice to sprinkle

3 tomatoes

2 red chillies

1 onion

1 sprig coriander

Freshly ground pepper

4 tbsp oil

100 g/3.5 oz chicken breast, cubed

1/2 green lettuce

75 g/2.5 fl oz double cream

Preparation time: approx. 45 minutes

Nutrition information per serving approx.: 12 g P, 19 g F, 28 g C, 355 kcal/1491 kJ

1 Sieve the flour onto the work surface and mix with the salt. Add approx. 70 ml/2.5 fl oz water and mix into a smooth dough. Form into 4 balls and leave to stand for approx. 20 minutes.

2 Cut the avocado flesh into small chunks and mash with a fork. Sprinkle with lemon juice.

3 Rinse and chop the tomatoes and mash with a fork. Finely chop the chillies. Peel the onion and cut into small cubes. Rinse the coriander, shake dry and pick off the leaves. Mix all the ingredients with the avocado and season with salt and pepper.

4 Roll the dough balls out into very thin flat loaves. Heat 2 tbsp oil in a frying pan and bake the 4 tacos, 2 minutes on each side.

5 Heat the remaining oil in a frying pan and fry the chicken cubes. Remove from pan and fill into the tacos. Arrange the lettuce, tacos and avocado sauce onto four plates. Garnish with a little double cream.

MEXICAN-STYLE SPICY CORN ON THE COB

1 Pre-heat the oven to 150 °C/300 °F/ gas mark 2. Place the chillies on a baking tray and roast for approx. 5 minutes on the middle rack. Then take out and leave to cool.

2 Remove the seeds and stalks from the chillies and chop them finely. Heat the butter in a saucepan and gently fry the onion and garlic. Add the chilli and pour in approx. 125 ml/4 fl oz water. Leave to simmer for about 20 minutes, until the dried chillies have turned soft.

3 Grill the corn on the cob, turning over regularly, until it turns a light yellow.

4 Puree the sauce and season to taste with salt, pepper and a little chilli powder. Remove the corn on the cob from the grill, sprinkle over salt, chilli powder and lime juice. Serve the corn on the cob with the sauce.

Finely chop the chillies.

Serves 4

3 dried chillies

2 tbsp butter

1 onion, chopped

1 clove garlic, crushed

4 fresh corn cobs, leaves removed

Salt

Freshly ground pepper

1 dash chilli powder

Lime juice for sprinkling

Preparation time: approx. 40 minutes

Nutrition information per serving approx.: 19 g P, 7 g F, 115 g C, 724 kcal/3041 kJ

STUFFED COURGETTE BLOSSOMS AU GRATIN

Mix chilli and minced meat.

Fry the meat.

Stir cream cheese into the meat.

1 Rinse the courgette flowers and pat dry. Cut out the core in the middle of the flowers. Peel and finely chop the onion. Trim and rinse the chillies, slit open, remove the seeds and finely chop the pod.

2 Mix the chopped chilli and onion with the minced meat and season to a pungent taste with salt, pepper and some chilli powder.

3 Heat the oil in a frying pan and stir-fry the meat for approx. 7 minutes. Pre-heat the oil in the deep fat fryer to 170 °C/340 °F.

4 Put the flour in one bowl and beat the egg in another bowl. Remove the minced meat from the pan and leave to cool.

5 Mix the minced meat with the cream cheese and fill this mixture into the courgette flowers.

6 Carefully twist up the tips of the courgette flowers. Dip the courgette flowers first into the egg and then roll them in the flour.

7 Sprinkle the stuffed courgette flowers with Parmesan and bake them in the deep fat fryer until they are golden brown. Serve with herbs and bell pepper slices.

■ **Serves 4**

8 courgette flowers

1 onion

2 red chillies

200 g/7 oz mixed minced meat

Salt

Freshly ground pepper

Chilli powder

2 tbsp oil

Oil for the deep fat fryer

3 tbsp flour

2 eggs

200 g/7 oz full fat cream cheese

50 ml/2 fl oz vegetable stock (cube)

80 g/2.75 oz grated Parmesan cheese

Herbs and bell pepper slices for garnishing

Preparation time: approx. 50 minutes

Nutrition information per serving approx.: 28 g P, 34 g F, 2 g C, 463 kcal/1944 kJ

Fill into the courgette flowers.

Twist together the flowers.

AVOCADO SORBET WITH TEQUILA CREAM

■ Serves 4

4 ripe avocados

1/2 cucumber

3 tbsp brown sugar

4 tbsp lemon juice

150 ml/5 fl oz cream

1 splash tequila

1/2 bunch lemon balm

Preparation time:
approx. 20 minutes

Time for freezing:
approx. 4 hours

Nutrition information
per serving approx.:
3 g P, 34 g F, 16 g C,
401 kcal/1687 kJ

1 Peel the avocados, cut into halves, remove the stone and cut the avocado into chunks.

2 Rinse and pat dry the cucumber and cut into cubes. Puree the avocado and cucumber with the sugar and 3 tbsp lemon juice with your electric hand whisk.

3 Put the sorbet in the freezer to get hard. In the meantime, mix the cream with tequila and the remaining lemon juice and whisk until stiff.

4 Remove the sorbet from the freezer and form dumplings with a serving spoon. Place these in a champagne bowl and serve with tequila cream and lemon balm garnish.

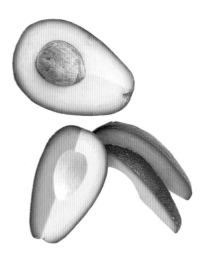

TAMALES STUFFED WITH BEANS AND CHILLI

1 Soak the maize leaves in warm water and leave to draw for approx. 3 hours.

2 Knead Masa Harina, pork lard, bicarbonate of soda, salt and chicken stock in a bowl and leave to stand for approx. 30 minutes.

3 Top and tail the beans, rinse and cut to chunks. Peel the onion and cut into cubes. Trim and rinse the chillies, slice open, remove the seeds and cut the pods into slices.

4 Heat the oil in a saucepan and stir in the onions, beans and chilli slices. Season to pungent taste with salt and pepper.

5 Remove the maize leaves from the water and pat dry. Place about 1 1/2 tbsp of the dough into the middle of each leaf and even out, leaving an edge on all sides. Now place approx. 1 1/2 tbsp of the bean paste onto the dough and wrap up the maize leaf. Press the leaves down a bit and fold up the ends of the leaves.

6 In a sauce pan, bring water to a boil, turn down the flame and steam the tamales over a low heat in the water for approx. 1 hour. They are ready when the dough does not stick to the leaf anymore when you unwrap it.

■ Serves 4

12 dried maize leaves (available in specialist shops)

500 g/17 oz Masa Harina (maize flour, available in specialist shops)

70 g/2.5 fl oz pork lard

2 tbsp bicarbonate of soda

1 tbsp salt

1/4 l/9 fl oz chicken stock (cube)

300 g/10 oz green beans

1 onion

2 red chillies

2 tbsp olive oil

Salt

Freshly ground pepper

Preparation time: approx. 2 hours

Standing time: approx. 3 hours

Nutrition information per serving approx.: 17 g P, 23 g F, 73 g C, 614 kcal/2579 kJ

SPICY TEX-MEX PIZZA POCKETS

■ **Serves 4**

1 bunch spring onions

2 packs frozen pizza dough (available in any supermarket)

8 tbsp chilli sauce or salsa verde (ready-made)

4 slices boiled ham

1 tin sweet corn (approx. 228 g/8 oz)

Salt

Freshly ground pepper

100 g/3.5 oz grated cheese

1 egg yolk for brushing

Preparation time: approx. 30 minutes

Nutrition information per serving approx.: 16 g P, 16 g F, 40 g C, 396 kcal/1666 kJ

1 Trim and rinse the spring onions and cut into rings. Roll out the pizza dough, cut in half and brush the salsa onto both halves.

2 Top the pizza dough with the spring onions and ham. Pre-heat the oven to 250 °C/480 °F/gas mark 9.

3 Drain the sweet corn and also spread over the pizza halves. Season with salt and pepper.

4 Sprinkle cheese over the pizza halves, then fold them up and press the edges firmly together.

5 Brush the pizza pockets with egg yolk and bake in the center oft the oven for approx. 10 minutes.

SPRING ONIONS

Spring onions are available throughout the year, but in spring their aroma is actually best.

■ *Since pizza pockets are very easy to prepare, they are especially suitable for parties or other special occasions. There are innumerable possible variations as concerns the ingredients that you fill into the pizza pockets. Why not try chicken breast with sweet corn and tomatoes, or fried minced beef with kidney beans and bell pepper.*

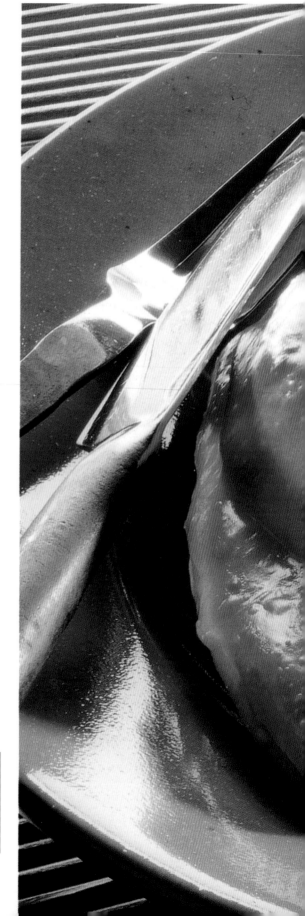

SALADS, SIDE DISHES, SAUCES AND VEGETABLES

Sauces are the A and O: they procure colour, aroma and an endless amount of possible variations. Just as salads, side dishes and vegetables, these should only be made of crisp and fresh ingredients.

HOME-MADE COLESLAW WITH CHILLI

■ Serves 4

1 white cabbage

1 red pepper

2 red chillies

1 red onion

3 tbsp balsamic vinegar

2 tbsp olive oil

Sugar

Salt

Freshly ground pepper

1 dash ground cumin

Preparation time:
approx. 20 minutes

Standing time:
approx. 1 hour

Nutrition information
3 g P, 8 g F, 14 g C,
149 kcal/626 kJ

1 Remove the outer leaves of the cabbage. Cut in half, remove the stalk and finely shred both halves.

2 Trim and rinse the red pepper, cut in two, remove seeds and cut into slices. Trim, rinse and finely chop the chillies.

3 Peel the onion and cut into rings. Mix vinegar with oil, sugar, salt, pepper and cumin.

4 Put white cabbage, onions, red pepper and chillies into a bowl and pour over the dressing. Leave to draw for approx. 1 hour.

Remove the stalk.

Finely shred the white cabbage.

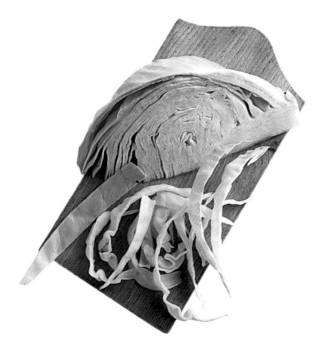

GUACAMOLE – MEXICAN AVOCADO PUREE

■ Serves 4

2 ripe avocados

2 tbsp lime juice

250 g/ 9 oz tomatoes

1 bunch spring onions

2 red chillies

1 red pepper

1/2 bunch parsley

1/2 bunch coriander

Salt

Freshly ground pepper

Taco chips for garnishing

Lime slices for garnishing

Preparation time: approx. 30 minutes

Nutrition information per serving approx.: 3 g P, 20 g F, 10 g C, 249 kcal/1045 kJ

1 Cut the avocados in two, remove the stone and spoon out the flesh. Sprinkle some lime juice over the flesh. Put the avocado peels aside. Mash the avocado flesh with an electric hand whisk.

2 Rinse the tomatoes, make a crosswise incision, dip them in simmering water, run under cold water, peel, then remove seeds and finely chop the tomatoes.

3 Trim and rinse the spring onions and cut into fine rings. Trim and rinse the chillies, remove the seeds and finely chop the pods. Trim and rinse the red pepper, remove seeds and also finely chop.

4 Rinse the herbs, shake dry and finely chop. Stir together the tomato with the spring onions, chillies, red pepper and herbs and add the remaining lime juice.

5 Add the pureed avocado. Fill the mixture into the avocado peels, arrange on plates with taco chips and lime slices.

■ *Guacamole is a basic element of Mexican cooking and is served with tacos, tortillas or bread.*

Remove the avocado stone.

Spoon out the flesh.

Mash the flesh.

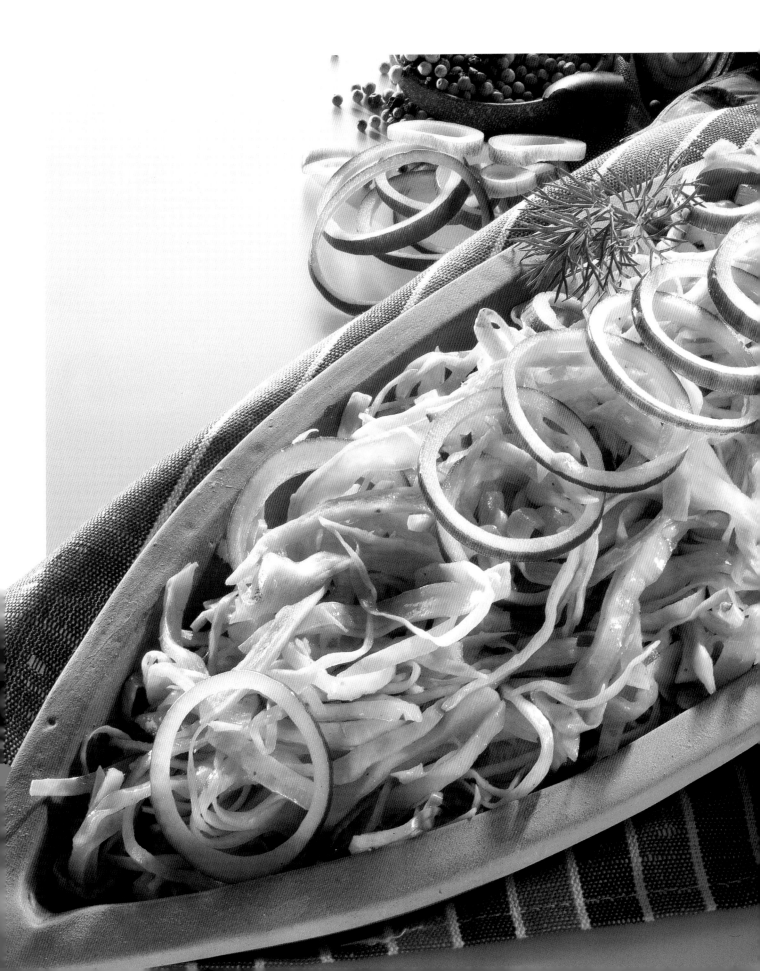

BELL PEPPERS WITH SWEET AND SPICY PINEAPPLE-CHILLI-STUFFING

SUGGESTED DRINK

A banana drink goes well with this dish. Per serving, mix 50 ml/2 fl oz banana juice with 2 tbsp gin and 100 ml/3 fl oz grapefruit juice; serve the drink with crushed ice.

■ Serves 4

1 baby pineapple

1 red onion

2 red peppers

1/4 bunch coriander

2 cloves garlic

3 tbsp lime juice

1/4 tsp ground caraway

150 g/5 oz grated Emmental cheese

8 bell peppers

Butter for the form

Preparation time: approx. 45 minutes

Nutrition information per serving approx.:
14 g, 12 g F, 22 g C, 272 kcal/1145 kJ

1 Peel the pineapple, cut out the eyes and the inedible central stalk, slice the pineapple and then cut into small chunks.

2 Peel and coarsely chop the onion. Trim and rinse the red pepper, slice open and remove the seeds, then cut into small slices.

3 Rinse the coriander and shake dry, then pick off the leaves. Peel and crush the garlic cloves. Pre-heat the oven to 180 °C/355 °F/gas mark 3.

4 In a bowl, mix the pineapple, onion, red pepper, coriander and garlic. Season with lime juice and caraway. Stir in the cheese.

5 Trim and rinse the bell peppers, cut off the lid and fill the mixture into the bell peppers. Brush an ovenproof dish with butter and place the bell peppers inside. Bake in the oven, on the middle rack, for approx. 15 minutes.

GRILLED AUBERGINES AND COURGETTES WITH SALSA

1 Peel and chop the onions. Peel and crush the garlic cloves. Rinse the herbs, shake dry and shred.

2 Peel and grate the ginger. Trim and rinse the red pepper, cut in two, remove the seeds and core and cut the pepper into slices.

3 Mix the pureed tomato with the prepared ingredients, season with salt and pepper.

4 Trim and rinse the aubergine and cut into slices. Sprinkle with salt. Trim and rinse the courgettes and also cut into slices.

5 Brush the salsa onto the vegetable slices and grill in the oven for approx. 8 minutes.

Brush the salsa onto the vegetables.

Serves 4

2 onions

2 cloves garlic

1/2 bunch lemon balm

1/2 bunch parsley

1 cm/.4" fresh ginger

2 red peppers

200 g/7 fl oz pureed tomatoes (pack)

Salt

Freshly ground pepper

600 g/1 lb 5 oz aubergines

600 g/1 lb 5 oz courgettes

Preparation time: approx. 30 minutes

Nutrition information per serving approx.: 6 g P, 9 g F, 14 g C, 174 kcal/733 kJ

GUACAMOLE –
MEXICAN AVOCADO PUREE

■ Serves 4

2 ripe avocados

2 tbsp lime juice

250 g/ 9 oz tomatoes

1 bunch spring onions

2 red chillies

1 red pepper

1/2 bunch parsley

1/2 bunch coriander

Salt

Freshly ground pepper

Taco chips for garnishing

Lime slices for garnishing

Preparation time: approx. 30 minutes

Nutrition information per serving approx.: 3 g P, 20 g F, 10 g C, 249 kcal/1045 kJ

1 Cut the avocados in two, remove the stone and spoon out the flesh. Sprinkle some lime juice over the flesh. Put the avocado peels aside. Mash the avocado flesh with an electric hand whisk.

2 Rinse the tomatoes, make a crosswise incision, dip them in simmering water, run under cold water, peel, then remove seeds and finely chop the tomatoes.

3 Trim and rinse the spring onions and cut into fine rings. Trim and rinse the chillies, remove the seeds and finely chop the pods. Trim and rinse the red pepper, remove seeds and also finely chop.

4 Rinse the herbs, shake dry and finely chop. Stir together the tomato with the spring onions, chillies, red pepper and herbs and add the remaining lime juice.

5 Add the pureed avocado. Fill the mixture into the avocado peels, arrange on plates with taco chips and lime slices.

■ *Guacamole is a basic element of Mexican cooking and is served with tacos, tortillas or bread.*

Remove the avocado stone.

Spoon out the flesh.

Mash the flesh.

Add the vegetables.

Fill the guacamole into the avocado peels.

TOMATO SAUCE WITH GREEN CHILLIES

Serves 4

4 beef tomatoes

3 green chillies

2 cloves garlic

1 onion

2 tbsp corn oil

50 ml/2 fl oz chicken stock (in jars)

Salt

Freshly ground pepper

1 bunch parsley

Preparation time: approx. 30 minutes

Nutrition information per serving approx.: 4 g P, 6 g F, 7 g C, 105 kcal/444 kJ

1 Rinse the tomatoes, make a crosswise incision, dip them in simmering water, run under cold water, peel and cut into cubes.

2 Rinse and finely chop the chillies. Peel and crush the garlic cloves. Peel and chop the onion.

3 Heat the oil in a saucepan and gently fry onion and garlic in it. Add tomatoes and chillies.

4 Add the chicken stock and season with salt and pepper. Finally, mash the sauce with your electric hand whisk.

5 Rinse and shake dry the parsley, finely chop and add to the sauce. Leave to draw for approx. 5 minutes. Serve garnished with herbs.

■ *This tomato sauce is especially good with home-made tortilla chips or other pastry dishes.*

SPICY AVOCADO-OLIVE PUREE

1 Peel the avocado, cut in two, remove the stone and cut the flesh in chunks. Drain the olives.

2 Rinse and trim the cherry tomatoes. Peel the onion and cut into cubes. Trim, rinse and finely chop the chilli.

3 Rinse the herbs, shake dry and finely chop.

4 Put avocado chunks, olives, tomatoes, onion and chilli into a bowl and mash with your electric hand whisk.

5 Stir in the herbs and season to taste with salt and pepper.

■ *The pungent avocado-olive puree can also be served hot. Fry the onions with the chilli and add the remaining ingredients after approx. 2 minutes. Finally, mash and season to taste.*

■ **Serves 4**

1 ripe avocado

100 g/3.5 oz black olives, stoned

4 cherry tomatoes

1 onion

1 red chilli

1/4 bunch coriander

1/4 bunch parsley

Salt

Freshly ground pepper

Preparation time: approx. 20 minutes

Nutrition information per serving approx.: 2 g P, 17 g F, 6 g C, 201 kcal/845 kJ

COLACHE – VEGETARIAN STEW

■ Serves 4

450 g/1 lb courgettes

2 corn on the cob

250 g/9 oz green beans

2 onions

2 cloves garlic

200 g/7 oz mixed bell peppers

4 tomatoes

2 red chillies

4 tbsp lard

Salt

Freshly ground pepper

Chilli powder

Preparation time:
approx. 40 minutes

Nutrition information
per serving approx.:
6 g P, 8 g F, 23 g C,
214 kcal/898 kJ

1 Trim and rinse the courgettes and cut into cubes. Trim and rinse the corn cobs and cut into rings.

2 Top and tail the beans and rinse them. Peel the onion and cut into rings. Peel and finely chop the garlic cloves.

3 Trim the bell peppers, rinse and cut into slices. Trim and rinse the tomatoes, make a crosswise incision, dip into simmering water, skin and remove the pips.

4 Trim, rinse and finely chop the chillies. Heat the lard in a saucepan and gently fry the vegetables in it. Season with salt, pepper and chilli powder.

5 Cover the saucepan and leave to simmer over a low heat for approx. 10 minutes.

COURGETTES

Small fruit of a size up to 20 cm/8″ are preferable. Their taste is much more aromatic than that of the larger courgettes.

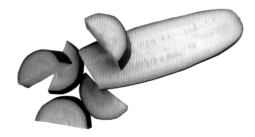

■ *Colache is one of the few vegetarian dishes in Mexican cooking. Vegetable is usually served as an accompaniment to fish, meat, poultry or other ingredients.*

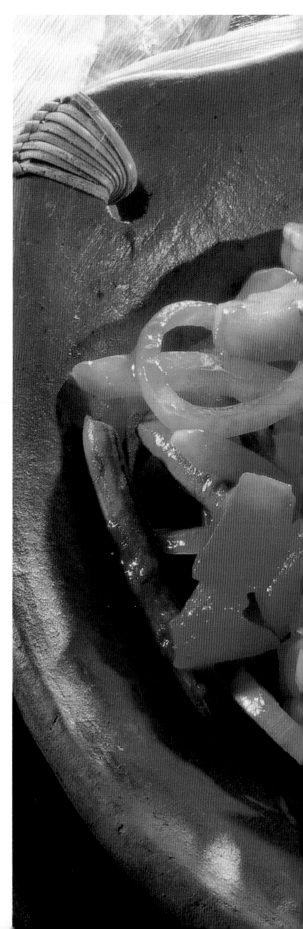

PUNGENT VEGETABLE STEW WITH SALAMI

Cut the bell pepper into chunks.

Cut the courgettes into slices.

1 Cut the bell peppers in two, remove core and seeds, rinse the fruit and cut into chunks.

2 Trim and rinse the courgettes and cut into slices. Rinse the tomatoes and cut into cubes.

3 Cut the bacon into small cubes, gently fry in a pan.

4 Add the vegetables and leave to simmer over a low heat for approx. 15 minutes.

5 Cut the turkey salami into cubes and add to the vegetables, stir in the salsa.

6 Leave to simmer for approx. 5 minutes. Season with salt and pepper. Serve the vegetable stew with French baguette.

▋ Serves 4

2 bell peppers

1 aubergine

2 courgettes

2 tomatoes

200 g/7 oz bacon

250 g/9 oz turkey salami

200 ml/7 fl oz chilli sauce (ready-made)

Salt, freshly ground pepper

Preparation time: approx. 30 minutes

Nutrition information per serving approx.: 32 g P, 28 g F, 8 g C, 452 kcal/1899 kJ

MEXICAN-TEXAN KING PRAWN SALAD

SUGGESTED DRINK

For this fruit drink,
mix 50 ml/2 fl oz cream with
100 ml/3 fl oz banana juice,
100 ml/3 fl oz grenadine and
a little crushed ice and serve
in tall glasses.

■ **Serves 4**

1 lettuce

**400 g/14 oz
king prawns with
head and tail**

Juice of 1 lime

1 tbsp olive oil

Salt

Freshly ground pepper

Chilli powder

3 hard-boiled eggs

3 tbsp mayonnaise

Preparation time:
approx. 20 minutes

Nutrition information
per serving approx.:
23 g P, 16 g F, 4 g C,
285 kcal/1198 kJ

1 Trim the lettuce, rinse the single leaves, pat dry and tear into mouth-size chunks.

2 Rinse the king prawns with cold water and sprinkle with lime juice.

3 Heat the oil in a pan and stir-fry the king prawns. Season with salt, pepper and chilli powder.

4 Peel the eggs, squash them with a fork and stir in the mayonnaise. Season to taste with a little lime juice.

5 Arrange the lettuce leaves on a plate, peel the prawns and place them on the lettuce. Serve garnished with a dash of egg mayonnaise.

MIXED ENSALADA FIESTA

1 Drain the kidney beans and sweet corn. Trim the bell peppers, cut in halves, remove core and seeds. Rinse, dry and cut the bell peppers in cubes.

2 Mix the prepared ingredients. Add the chilli sauce, stir well and leave to draw.

3 Arrange the salad on plates and garnish with tortilla chips.

Add the chilli sauce.

■ **Serves 4**

1 tin kidney beans (425 ml/15 fl oz)

1 tin sweet corn (425 ml/15 fl oz)

1 green bell pepper

1 red bell pepper

200 ml/7 fl oz chilli sauce (ready-made)

Tortilla chips

Preparation time: approx. 15 minutes

Nutrition information per serving approx.: 8 g P, 2 g F, 38 g C, 205 kcal/855 kJ

MIXED SALAD WITH FRESH SALMON FILLET

■ Serves 4

600 g/1 lb 5 oz salmon fillet

Salt

Freshly ground pepper

2 tbsp lemon juice

4 tbsp olive oil

1 small red bell pepper

11 small yellow bell pepper

1 red onion

1 clove garlic

100 g/3.5 oz black olives, stoned

2 tbsp capers

1 lime

Lettuce leaves for garnishing

Preparation time: approx. 40 minutes

Standing time: approx. 10 minutes

Nutrition information per serving approx.: 34 g P, 35 g F, 14 g C, 553 kcal/2322 kJ

1 Pre-heat the oven to 250 °C/480 °F/ gas mark 9. Rinse and dry the salmon fillet and cut into slices. Season with salt and pepper and sprinkle with lemon juice.

2 Brush an ovenproof dish with olive oil, place the fish in it and sprinkle with approx. 1 tbsp olive oil. Cook in the oven for approx. 10 minutes, on the middle rack. Remove the fish and leave to cool.

3 Trim and halve the bell peppers, de-seed, rinse and then cut into slices.

4 Peel the onion and cut into rings. Peel and finely chop the garlic clove. Drain the olives and cut into rings.

5 In a bowl, mix bell pepper slices, onion rings, garlic, olives and capers. Halve the lime, squeeze and grate some of the lime peel. Stir lime peel, lime juice, remaining oil, salt and pepper into a dressing.

6 Rinse and dry the lettuce leaves and arrange on four plates. Add the salad ingredients, then the fish and pour over the dressing. Leave to draw for approx. 10 minutes and then serve.

Cut the fish into slices.

Sprinkle olive oil over the fish.

Cut the olives into rings.

Mix the salad ingredients.

Pour over the dressing.

RED CHILLI SAUCE WITH HERBS

Serves 4

6 dried green chillies

1 onion

2 tbsp olive oil

1 tin tomatoes (480 ml/16 fl oz)

2 cloves garlic

2 tsp sugar

1/2 tsp salt

Freshly ground pepper

1/2 tsp turmeric

1/4 bunch oregano

Preparation time: approx. 45 minutes

Standing time: approx. 15 minutes

Nutrition information per serving approx.: 2 g P, 10 g F, 12 g C, 156 kcal/657 kJ

1 Soak the chillies in water for approx. 15 minutes. Then remove the chillies and pat dry.

2 Finely chop the chillies. Peel and coarsely chop the onion.

3 Heat the oil in a sauce pan and gently fry the onion and chillies. Add the tomatoes with the juice. Add the peeled and crushed garlic cloves. Bring to a boil, stirring constantly.

4 Squash with a fork and season to taste with sugar, salt, pepper and turmeric.

5 Wash and shake dry the oregano and pick off the leaves. Pour the sauce into a bowl and garnish with oregano leaves.

■ *This chilli sauce goes well with a maize loaf or other home-made Texan-Mexican bakery goods.*

MEXICAN SWEET POTATO-AVOCADO SALSA

1 Peel the sweet potato and cut into medium-sized chunks. Trim, rinse and halve the bell pepper, remove seeds and then cut into cubes.

2 Peel and coarsely chop the onion. Trim, rinse and finely chop the chillies.

3 Peel and halve the avocado, remove the stone and cut the flesh into cubes.

4 Mix all ingredients in a bowl, adding lemon and orange juice.

5 Rinse and shake dry the lemon balm, pull off the leaves and stir them into the salsa. Leave to draw for approx. 1 hour.

■ Serves 4

1 sweet potato

1 red bell pepper

1 yellow bell pepper

1 red onion

2 red chillies

1 avocado

2 tbsp lemon juice

4 tbsp orange juice

1/4 bunch lemon balm

Preparation time: approx. 40 minutes

Standing time: approx. 1 hour

Nutrition information
6 g P, 11 g F, 42 g C,
312 kcal/1312 kJ

SOUPS AND STEWS

Many of these hearty dishes were developed on the big cattle trails in the Southwestern USA. Here you can discover what else Tex-Mex cooking has to offer other than chilli con carne.

LIME SOUP WITH EGG AND HERBS

■ **Serves 4**

3 egg yolks
125 ml/4 fl oz milk
Freshly ground nutmeg
2 tbsp lime juice
3 small onions
2 celery stalks
3 carrots
2 tbsp butter
600 ml/1 pint 1 fl oz chicken stock (jar)
Salt
Freshly ground pepper
1/2 bunch parsley
1/2 bunch dill
Herbs for garnishing

Preparation time: approx. 40 minutes

Nutrition information per serving approx.: 23 g P, 25 g F, 8 g C, 382 kcal/1604 kJ

1 In a bowl, mix the egg yolks with milk, a little nutmeg and the lime juice.

2 Brush a cup or ovenproof dish with a little butter. Cover the egg mixture and gently cook in a bain-marie for approx. 30 minutes; the water should be hot but not boiling.

3 Peel the onions and cut into rings. Trim and rinse the celery and cut into chunks. Trim, peel, rinse and slice the carrots.

4 Heat the butter in a saucepan, gently fry the onions. Add celery and carrots.

5 Pour the chicken stock over and season with salt and pepper. Leave to simmer over a low heat for approx. 20 minutes. Rinse and shake dry the herbs, finely chop them and add to the soup.

6 Turn the egg out of the cup or dish and cut into small cubes. Spoon onto four plates and then add the hot soup. Garnish with herbs and serve hot.

LIMES

The flesh of limes has double the amount of juice that lemons have and is usually without pips. In warm countries, the sour limes provide welcome refreshment.

ANTONIO'S VEGETABLE STEW WITH HARICOT BEANS

Serves 4

300 g/10 oz
dried haricot beans

1 l/1 quart vegetable
stock (cube)

800 g/1 lb 12 oz
soup bones

4 carrots

2 onions

1 red chilli

1 green chilli

250 g/9 oz courgettes

250 g/9 oz celery stalks

1 bunch parsley

Salt, ground pepper

Preparation time:
approx. 1 1/2 hours
Standing time:
one night

Nutrition information
per serving approx.:
19 g P, 3 g F, 41 g C,
291 kcal/1224 kJ

1 Soak the beans over night in approx. 300 ml/10 fl oz water. Drain well.

2 Heat the chicken stock in a saucepan and add the soup bones to draw for approx. 30 minutes.

3 Trim, peel and rinse the carrots and cut into slices. Peel the onions and cut into rings. Trim and rinse the chillies, cut in two, remove seeds and finely chop the pods.

4 Trim and rinse the courgettes and cut into slices. Trim, rinse and chop the celery stalks.

5 Rinse and shake dry the parsley, then finely chop. Remove the soup bones from the stock. Add the haricot beans, onions and chillies and simmer for approx. 1 hour. After 40 minutes, add the remaining vegetables and cook for another 20 minutes.

6 Season the soup with salt and pepper, spoon out and serve garnished with parsley.

Let the soup bones draw.

Add the vegetables to the soup.

BLACK BEAN STEW

SUGGESTED DRINK

To make a fresh lemonade, you need the juice of 1/2 lime, 40 g/1.5 oz caster sugar and 150 ml/5 fl oz mineral water. Mix and serve chilled.

Serves 4

500 g/17 oz dried black beans

approx. 500 g/17 oz pickled pork

1 red chilli

Tabasco sauce

Salt

Freshly ground pepper

8 slices air-dried ham, f. ex. Spanish Serrano

Preparation time:
approx. 3 hours

Standing time:
approx. 18 hours

Nutrition information per serving approx.:
30 g P, 5 g F, 60 g C,
421 kcal/1768 kJ

1 Soak the beans in water for approx. 18 hours. Drain well.

2 Cook the beans in 2 1/2 quarts of water for approx. 2 minutes. Reduce heat and leave to simmer over a low heat for approx. 2 hours.

3 Rinse and pat dry the pickled pork, add to the beans and simmer for another 50 minutes. Trim, rinse, halve, de-seed and finely chop the chilli.

4 Remove the pickled pork, cut the meat off the bone and stir into the soup again, adding the chilli.

5 Season to taste with Tabasco sauce, salt and pepper. Form the ham slices into little rolls. Spoon the soup into four dishes and garnish with the ham rolls.

CHILLED VEGETABLE SOUP WITH CHILLIES

1 Rinse the tomatoes, make a crosswise incision, dip in simmering water, skin, chop and purée with your electric hand whisk.

2 Peel and chop the onion. Rinse the chillies, cut in two, remove the seeds and chop the pods.

3 Peel and crush the garlic. Trim and rinse the bell peppers, cut in halves, de-seed and cut into slices.

4 Drain the sweet corn. Place all of the vegetables in a soup bowl. Pour the tomato juice over the vegetables.

5 Stir in vinegar and oil and leave to chill in the fridge for at least 30 minutes. Before serving, season to taste with salt and pepper. Spoon onto four plates and sprinkle parsley on top.

Pour over the tomato juice.

Serves 4

750 g/1 lb 10 oz ripe tomatoes

1 red onion

2 red chillies

1 clove garlic

1 red bell pepper

1 green bell pepper

150 g/5 oz sweet corn (tin)

250 ml/9 fl oz chilled tomato juice

3 tbsp olive oil

3 tbsp red wine vinegar

Salt

Freshly ground pepper

2 tbsp chopped parsley

Preparation time: approx. 40minutes

Standing time: approx. 30 minutes

Nutrition information per serving approx.: 19 g P, 7 g F, 15 g C, 724 kcal/3041 kJ

PUMPKIN TOMATO SOUP MEXICAN STYLE

■ Serves 4

2 dried red chillies

1 onion

1 clove garlic

2 tbsp butter

500 ml/17 fl oz chicken stock (jar)

3 tomatoes

250 g/9 oz pumpkin chunks (tin)

80 g/2.75 oz sour cream

Salt

Freshly ground pepper

Herbs for garnishing

Preparation time: approx. 30 minutes

Standing time: approx. 1 hour

Nutrition information per serving approx.: 16 g P, 21 g F, 6 g C, 299 kcal/1258 kJ

1 Soak the chillies in water for approx. 1 hour, drain, de-seed and then finely chop.

2 Peel and chop the onion. Peel and finely chop the garlic clove.

3 Heat the butter in a saucepan and gently fry onion, garlic and chillies.

4 Pour over chicken stock and approx. 200 ml/7 fl oz water. Leave to simmer for approx. 10 minutes.

5 Rinse the tomatoes, make a crosswise incision, dip in simmering water, skin and chop. Drain the pumpkin chunks. Add tomatoes and pumpkin to the soup approx. 5 minutes before the end of cooking time.

6 Stir in the sour cream and season to taste with salt and pepper.

7 Spoon out onto four plates and garnish with herbs.

Finely chop the chillies.

Gently fry chillies and onion.

Pour over the stock.

Add the vegetables.

Stir in the sour cream.

CHILLED AVOCADO SOUP WITH LIMES

Serves 4

3 ripe avocados

1 onion

375 ml/13 fl oz vegetable stock (cube)

3 tbsp sherry

3 tbsp lime juice

Salt

Freshly ground pepper

1 red pepper

80 g/2.75 oz crème fraîche

Grated lime peel

1 tbsp chopped parsley

Preparation time: approx. 20 minutes

Standing time: approx. 2 hours

Nutrition information per serving approx.: 3 g P, 36 g F, 7 g C, 390 kcal/1638 kJ

1 Peel and halve the avocados, remove the stone and cut the avocados into chunks.

2 Peel and finely chop the onion. Purée the avocados with your electric hand whisk.

3 Stir in the vegetable stock, sherry and lime juice. Season to taste with salt and pepper.

4 Trim and rinse the pepper, cut in two, de-seed and cut into slices. Add the pepper and chopped onion to the soup.

5 Stir in the crème fraîche. Leave to draw in the fridge for approx. 2 hours. Arrange the soup on plates and garnish with lemon peel and parsley.

TORTILLA SOUP WITH CRÈME FRAÎCHE

1 Heat the oil in a deep fat fryer. Trim and rinse the tomatoes and gently fry in an oil-free frying pan. Season with salt and pepper.

2 Coarsely crumble the tortillas and fry in the deep fat fryer until golden brown.

3 Peel the onions and cut into rings. Peel and finely chop the garlic.

4 Heat the lard in a saucepan and gently fry the onions and garlic. Add the tomatoes and season with salt, pepper and chilli powder.

5 Pour over the chicken stock and blend the ingredients with your electric hand whisk. Simmer the soup over a low heat for approx. 20 minutes.

6 Peel the avocado, cut into slices and sprinkle with the lemon juice. Spoon out the soup and serve garnished with avocado slices, tortilla chips, crème fraîche and parsley leaves.

Serves 4

Oil for deep fat frying

3 tomatoes

Salt

Freshly ground pepper

12 maize tortillas

2 onions

2 cloves garlic

2 tbsp lard

Chilli powder

1 l/1 quart chicken stock (cube)

1/2 avocado

Some lemon juice

80 g/2.5 fl oz crème fraîche

Parsley leaves for garnishing

Preparation time: approx. 40 minutes

Nutrition information per serving approx.: 2 g P, 21 g F, 5 g C, 228 kcal/957 kJ

CHICKEN SOUP WITH LEMON AND TORTILLA CHIPS

■ **Serves 4**

2 onions

1 green chilli

1 red chilli

2 cloves garlic

1 beef tomato

200 g/7 oz chicken breast

2 tbsp olive oil

Salt

Freshly ground pepper

600 ml/1 pint 1 fl oz chicken stock (in a jar)

Grated peel of one organic lemon

Some lemon juice

180 g/6 oz tortilla chips

Herbs for garnishing

Preparation time: approx. 40 minutes

Nutrition information per serving approx.: 29 g P, 16 g F, 5 g C, 322 kcal/1355 kJ

1 Peel and chop the onion. Trim and rinse the chillies, slice open and remove seeds and cut the chillies into fine rings.

2 Peel and finely chop the garlic. Rinse the tomatoes, make a crosswise incision, dip into simmering water, skin and chop.

3 Rinse the chicken breast, pat dry and cut into slices.

4 Heat the oil in a saucepan, gently fry onions and chillies. Add the garlic. Season with salt and pepper. Add the chicken stock.

5 Stir in the meat and leave to simmer over a low heat for approx. 15 minutes.

6 Just before the end of cooking time has been reached, add the lemon peel and lemon juice and season to taste. Spoon out the soup onto four plates, and serve garnished with tortilla chips and herbs.

TORTILLA CHIPS

These are amongst the most well-known specialities of Mexican cooking. The chips are predominantly made of maize flour.

■ *This chicken soup with lemon and tortilla chips is very easy to prepare and thus well suited for festive occasions. It is bound to be a party hit that everyone will recommend.*

PORK STEW "RAMONA"

■ Serves 4

150 g/5 oz long-grain rice

Salt

3 carrots

2 small courgettes

2 cloves garlic

1 onion

300 g/10 oz shoulder of pork

2 tbsp olive oil

Freshly ground pepper

700 ml/1 pint 7 fl oz vegetable stock (cube)

1/2 bunch oregano

2 tbsp chopped parsley

Preparation time: approx. 1 hour

Nutrition information per serving approx.: 16 g P, 24 g F, 36 g C, 459 kcal/1929 kJ

1 Cook the rice in lightly salted water for approx. 15 minutes. Drain and keep in a warm place. Trim, peel and rinse the carrots and cut them into slices. Trim and rinse the courgettes, cut in halves and also into slices.

2 Peel and finely chop the garlic. Peel and chop the onion. Rinse the meat, pat dry and cut into strips.

3 Heat the oil in a saucepan and gently fry the onion and garlic. Add the carrots and courgettes. Season thoroughly with salt and pepper.

4 Pour the stock and approx. 150 ml/ 5 fl oz water over the vegetables. Add the meat and simmer over a low heat for approx. 20 minutes.

5 Rinse and shake dry the oregano, pick off the leaves and add them to the soup shortly before the end of cooking time.

6 Spoon the rice out onto four plates, pour the soup over and serve hot.

Gently fry onion and garlic.

Add the vegetables.

COLOURFUL GARLIC SOUP WITH ALMONDS AND HERBS

SUGGESTED DRINK

To make a Sangrita, measure out 100 ml/3 fl oz tomato juice per person and mix this with 1 tbsp orange juice, 1 dash of lemon juice, salt, pepper and a dash of Tabasco sauce.

■ **Serves 4**

2 dry rolls

100 g/3.5 oz almonds

4 cloves garlic

1 red bell pepper

3 tbsp olive oil

3 tbsp sherry vinegar

1/2 l/17 fl oz iced water

Salt, freshly ground black pepper

1 bunch basil leaves for garnishing

1 tbsp ground mixed pepper

Preparation time: approx. 45 minutes

Standing time: approx. 30 minutes

Nutrition information per serving approx.: 7 g P, 13 g F, 18 g C, 240 kcal/1010 kJ

1 Soak the dry rolls in water, drain and squeeze out excess liquid.

2 Pour boiling water over the almonds and skin them. Peel the garlic and cut into rings.

3 Trim and rinse the bell pepper, halve, de-seed and cut into slices.

4 Blend rolls, almonds and garlic, topped with vinegar and oil, with your electric hand whisk.

5 Give this mixture into a bowl and pour the iced water over it. Season to taste with salt and black pepper and place in the fridge for approx. 30 minutes. Stir in the bell pepper slices.

6 Rinse and shake dry the basil leaves and cut them into slices.

7 Serve out the soup. Garnish with basil leaves and ground mixed pepper.

MEXICAN SWEET CORN STEW WITH RIBS

1 Rinse and pat dry the meat, cut into chunks and rub with salt and pepper.

2 Heat the vegetable stock in a saucepan and draw the meat in it for approx. 30 minutes.

3 Drain the sweet corn. Trim and rinse the chillies, halve, remove the seeds and finely chop the chilli pods.

4 Rinse, shake dry and mince the coriander. Peel and chop the onions. Peel and finely chop the garlic cloves.

5 Add the sweet corn, chillies, coriander, onions and garlic to the meat. Leave to simmer over a low heat for approx. 15 minutes.

6 Spoon the sweet corn stew onto four plates and serve.

Cut the meat into chunks.

■ **Serves 4**

1 kg/2 lb 3 oz pork ribs

Salt

Freshly ground pepper

1 l/1 quart vegetable stock (cube)

500 g/17 oz sweet corn (tinned)

2 red chillies

1/4 bunch coriander

3 onions

4 cloves garlic

Preparation time: approx. 50 minutes

Nutrition information per serving approx.: 42 g P, 77 g F, 30 g C, 1054 kcal/4428 kJ

SPICY MEATBALL SOUP WITH HERBS

Serves 4

1 egg

1 red chilli

1 onion

500 g/17 oz mixed minced meat

Salt

Freshly ground pepper

Chilli powder

3 tbsp olive oil

4 pickled peppers

1/4 bunch coriander

725 ml/1 pint 6 fl oz vegetable stock (cube)

1 bay leaf

Freshly ground nutmeg

80 g/2.75 oz croutons

Preparation time: approx. 1 hour

Nutrition information per serving approx.: 26 g P, 44 g F, 2 g C, 554 kcal/232 kJ

1 Beat the egg in a bowl. Trim and rinse the chilli, cut in half, de-seed and cut the chilli into slices. Peel and chop the onion.

2 Mix the minced meat with the onion, chilli and egg. Season with salt, pepper and chilli powder, wet your hands and form the mixture into small balls.

3 Heat the oil in a frying pan and fry the meatballs on all sides for approx. 5 minutes.

4 Drain and chop the peppers. Rinse and shake dry the herbs and pick off the leaves.

5 Heat the vegetable stock in a saucepan, add pepper, herbs and bay leaf. Season with nutmeg.

6 Remove the meatballs from the pan, pat dry with a tea towel and add them to the soup. Simmer over a low heat for approx. 20 minutes.

7 Spoon out the soup onto four plates and serve garnished with croutons.

Knead the minced meat.

Form the mixture into balls.

Fry the meatballs.

Pat dry the meatballs.

Add the meatballs to the soup.

EGGS, RICE, NOODLES, POTATOES AND SWEET CORN

Here, traditional foodstuffs are used to prepare the most unusual dishes. In Southwestern USA, they are served to accompany a large variety of meals.

MEXICAN-STYLE FILLED PASTRY WRAPS

Serves 4

100 g/3.5 oz flour

Flour for the work surface

Salt

1 tsp caster sugar

6 tbsp olive oil

2 eggs

1500 g/3 lb spring cabbage

1 bunch spring onions

2 tbsp butter

Freshly ground pepper

50 g/1.75 oz cashew nuts

100 g/3.5 oz sultanas

Fat for the deep fat fryer

100 ml/3 fl oz chilli sauce (ready-made)

Preparation time: approx. 40 minutes

Standing time: approx. 15 minutes

Nutrition information per serving approx.: 18 g P, 30 g F, 51 g C, 578 kcal/2428 kJ

1 Sieve the flour onto a work surface, form a mould in the centre. Pour 1/2 tsp salt, the caster sugar, olive oil, 1 egg and 400 ml/14 fl oz water into the mould. Knead into a smooth dough and form a ball.

2 Cover the dough and leave to rest in a cool place for approx. 15 minutes. Line a baking tray with greaseproof paper.

3 Trim, rinse and finely shred the spring cabbage. Trim and rinse the spring onions and cut into rings. Heat the butter in a frying pan and gently fry the cabbage and spring onions for approx. 5 minutes. Season with salt and pepper. Stir in cashew nuts and sultanas. Preheat the oven to 225 °C/435 °F/gas mark 7.

4 Divide the dough into 16 portions and roll out each one into a flat loaf of approx. 15 cm Ø. Spread the vegetable on the flat cakes and flap over to form a half moon. Press the edges together thoroughly.

5 Heat the fat in the deep fat fryer. Beat the remaining egg in a bowl and brush over the pastry wraps. Bake in the deep fat fryer until golden brown. Serves the pastries with chilli sauce.

GREEN RICE WITH ONIONS AND CHILLIES

1 Soak the rice in warm water for approx. 5 minutes. Trim and rinse the spinach. Place it in a saucepan over medium heat and quickly let it cook down.

2 Rinse and shake dry the parsley and mince the leaves. Peel the onions, chop one and cut the others into rings. Peel and crush the garlic.

3 Blend the spinach with garlic and 125 ml/4 fl oz water with your electric hand whisk. Add chopped onion and parsley. Heat the oil in a frying pan, add the rice and gently fry for 5 minutes.

4 After 2 minutes, pour off the excess oil. Add the spinach mixture and leave to draw for approx. 2 minutes. Add 750 ml/

1 pint 7 fl oz hot water, bring to the boil and then simmer over a medium heat for approx. 15 minutes. Preheat the oven to 180 °C/355 °F/gas mark 4.

5 Heat the butter in a frying pan and gently fry the remaining onions. Rinse the chillies, slice open, de-seed, finely chop and add to the onions. Leave to draw for approx. 5 minutes.

6 Brush an ovenproof dish with butter and fill it with alternating layers of rice and onions. Top with cheese and crème fraîche. Cook in the centre of the oven for approx. 10 minutes.

■ **Serves 4**

200 g/7 oz long-grain rice

150 g/5 oz spinach

1 bunch parsley

8 onions

1 clove garlic

125 ml/4 fl oz oil

Salt

30 g/1 oz butter

3 red chillies

125 g/4.5 oz grated Gouda or Cheddar, medium flavour

125 g/4.5 fl oz crème fraîche

Preparation time: approx. 1 hour

Nutrition information per serving approx.: 16 g P, 47 g F, 53 g C, 733 kcal/3081 kJ

MIXED RICE WITH AVOCADO SAUCE

■ **Serves 4**

2 onions

2 cloves garlic

200 g/7 oz country rice (rice mixture available in organic shops)

4 tbsp corn oil

Salt

Freshly ground pepper

400 ml/14 fl oz chicken stock (in a jar)

2 carrots

1 green chilli

1 ripe avocado

3 tbsp olive oil

Lime juice

Herbs for garnishing

Preparation time: approx. 40 minutes

Nutrition information per serving approx.: 17 g P, 24 g F, 42 g C, 487 kcal/2046 kJ

1 Peel the onions and cut into rings. Peel and finely chop the garlic. Rinse the rice in cold water and drain.

2 Heat the corn oil in a saucepan and gently fry the onions and garlic. Add the rice and fry for approx. 5 minutes. Season with salt and pepper.

3 Pour in the chicken stock, bring to the boil and leave the rice mixture to simmer for approx. 20 minutes.

4 Trim, peel and rinse the carrots and cut them into slices. Trim and rinse the chilli, cut in two, remove the seeds and chop it.

5 Peel the avocado, remove the stone and cut the flesh into chunks. Blend the carrots, chilli and avocado with the oil and some lime juice with your electric hand whisk. Season with salt and pepper.

6 Drain the rice and serve on plates with the avocado sauce. Season with salt and pepper.

COUNTRY RICE MIXTURE

Country rice is a mix of red rice, wild rice and brown rice. It is available in organic and health-food shops.

POTATO GRATIN WITH CHILLIES AND BACON

Serves 4

1 kg/2 lb 3 oz potatoes

2 red chillies

2 onions

2 tbsp butter

Salt

Freshly ground pepper

Chilli powder

Butter for the dish

100 g/3.5 oz bacon

150 g/5 oz grated Gruyère cheese

180 g/6 oz crème fraîche

Herbs for garnishing

Preparation time: approx.1 1/4 hours

Nutrition information per serving approx.: 12 g P, 32 g F, 48 g C, 614 kcal/2580 kJ

1 Wash and peel the potatoes and cut into slices. Trim and rinse the chillies, cut in two, de-seed and finely chop them. Peel the onions and cut into rings.

2 Heat the butter in a frying pan and gently fry the potatoes, chilli and onions.

3 Season to taste with salt, pepper and chilli powder. In the meantime, brush an ovenproof dish with butter. Preheat the oven to 180 °C/355 °F/gas mark 4.

4 Slice the bacon. Fill the dish with the fried potato mixture and then spread the bacon over. Top with cheese, then brush with the crème fraîche.

5 Cook in the centre of the oven for approx. 40 minutes. Serve the potato gratin garnished with herbs.

Layer the potatoes in a dish.

Spread the bacon over them.

SPICY TURKEY LASAGNE WITH TOMATOES

SUGGESTED DRINK

For one cup of Mexican-style coffee, boil 125 ml/4.5 fl oz water, 1/4 cinnamon stick, 1 clove, 20 g/scant 1 oz caster sugar and 2 heaped tbsp of ground coffee for approx. 5 minutes. Pour through a sieve before serving in a glass.

■ **Serves 4**

1 turkey chop, approx. 800 g/ 1 lb 12 oz

1 onion

2 cloves garlic

750 ml/1 pint 7 fl oz chicken stock (in a jar)

500 g/17 oz tomatoes

2 red chillies

1/4 bunch thyme

1/4 bunch oregano

2 tbsp butter

Salt

Freshly ground pepper

200 g/7 oz lasagne pasta (not pre-cooked)

150 g/5 oz grated Cheddar or Gouda, medium flavour

Preparation time: approx. 1 1/2 hours

Nutrition information per serving approx.: 69 g P, 27 g F, 42 g C, 758 kcal/3184 kJ

1 Rinse and pat dry the turkey chop. Peel and chop the onion. Peel and finely chop the garlic.

2 Heat the chicken stock in a saucepan. Add the turkey chop with the onion and half the garlic and simmer for approx. 1 hour.

3 Trim, rinse and slice the tomatoes. Trim and rinse the chillies, cut in two, de-seed and finely chop. Rinse and shake dry the herbs and mince them.

4 Heat the butter in a frying pan and gently fry the remaining garlic. Add tomatoes, chillies and herbs. Season well with salt and pepper. Preheat the oven to 180 °C/355 °F/gas mark 4.

5 Remove the meat, pat dry and cut slices of meat off the bone. Brush an ovenproof dish with butter. Fill in the lasagne pasta, meat and tomatoes in alternating layers. Cover with grated cheese and bake in the centre of the oven for approx. 15 minutes.

FOAMY OMELETTES WITH CHEESE SAUCE

1 In a bowl, beat the eggs with the mineral water; season with salt, pepper and nutmeg.

2 Trim and rinse the chillies, cut in two, de-seed and cut into rings. Make a crosswise incision in the tomato skins, dip them in simmering water, skin and chop them.

3 Peel and chop the onion. Heat 2 tbsp butter in a saucepan and gently fry the onions. Add chillies and tomatoes. Season with salt and pepper and add the stock. Stir in the cream and then the cheese. Keep the sauce warm.

4 Heat the remaining butter in a frying pan and bake the four omelettes one after another. Arrange the omelettes on plates and spoon over the cheese sauce.

Stir in the cheese.

■ **Serves 4**

12 eggs

50 ml/2 fl oz sparkling mineral water

Salt

Freshly ground pepper

1 red chilli

1 green chilli

3 tomatoes

1 onion

6 tbsp butter

75 ml/2.5 fl oz vegetable stock (cube)

2 tbsp cream

150 g/5 oz grated Cheddar cheese

50 g/1.75 oz tortilla chips

Preparation time: approx. 40 minutes

Nutrition information per serving approx.: 32 g P, 39 g F, 4 g C, 540 kcal/2269 kJ

SHELL NOODLES WITH MEXICAN FILLING

■ Serves 4

500 g/17 oz oyster mushrooms

1 clove garlic

1 onion

3 tomatoes

6 pickled green peppers

2 tbsp butter

Salt

Freshly ground pepper

80 g/2.75 oz tomato ketchup

1 tbsp chilli sauce (ready-made)

Chilli powder, butter for the dish

250 g/9 oz large shell noodles

200 ml/7 fl oz vegetable stock (cube)

80 g/2.75 grated Emmentaler cheese

Preparation time: approx. 20 minutes

Nutrition information per serving approx.: 10 g P, 5 g F, 44 g C, 284 kcal/1192 kJ

1 Trim, rinse and chop the oyster mushrooms. Peel and crush the garlic. Peel and chop the onion.

2 Rinse the tomatoes, make a crosswise incision, dip them in simmering water, skin and cut them into cubes.

3 Drain the peppers and chop them. Heat the butter in a saucepan and gently fry the onion. Add garlic and oyster mushrooms and keep on frying gently. Season with salt and pepper.

4 Add the tomatoes, peppers and ketchup. Season with chilli sauce, chilli powder, salt and pepper. Preheat the oven to 180 °C/355 °F/gas mark 4. Brush an ovenproof dish with a little butter.

5 Fill the noodles with the mushroom mixture and place them in the dish. Pour over the vegetable stock. Sprinkle with cheese, cover and cook in the centre of the oven for approx. 10 minutes. Remove cover and cook for another 20 minutes approx.

Chop the oyster mushrooms.

Add the oyster mushrooms.

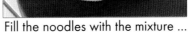

Stir in the tomatoes.

Fill the noodles with the mixture ...

... and sprinkle with cheese.

RICE WITH CHICKEN BREAST AND SPICY WALNUT SAUCE

Serves 4

200 g/7 oz
whole grain rice

Salt

500 g/17 oz
chicken breast fillet

750 ml/1 pint 7 fl oz
vegetable stock
(in a jar)

2 slices white bread

100 g/3.5 oz
walnut kernels

1 red chilli

1 onion

2 tbsp butter

Freshly ground pepper

1 clove garlic

Chopped chives,
parsley leaves and
chilli pods for
garnishing

Preparation time:
approx. 40 minutes

Nutrition information
per serving approx.:
37 g P, 18 g F, 41 g C,
510 kcal/2144 kJ

1 Cook the rice in salted water for approx. 30 minutes. Rinse and dry the meat and cut into strips.

2 Heat the vegetable stock in a saucepan and simmer the meat in it for approx. 8 minutes. Remove the meat with a skimmer and drain, then keep in a warm place.

3 Cut the white bread into small pieces. Coarsely chop the walnuts. Trim and rinse the chilli, de-seed and finely chop. Peel and finely chop the onion.

4 Heat the butter in a frying pan and gently fry the onion. Add chilli, bread and walnuts. Season with salt and pepper. Peel and crush the garlic and add to the rest. Gently stir-fry.

5 Pour 80 ml/2.5 fl oz of the vegetable stock over the chilli paste and leave to draw for approx. 4 minutes. Then blend the mixture with your electric hand whisk.

6 Drain the rice, arrange rice and meat on plates, spoon over the chilli paste and serve garnished with herbs and red chillies.

FRUITY RICE CASSEROLE MEXICAN STYLE

1 Cook the rice in salted water for approx. 20 minutes. Rinse the tomatoes, make a crosswise incision, dip in simmering water, skin and cut into cubes.

2 Peel the onion and cut into rings. Peel and crush the garlic.

3 Trim and rinse the peppers, cut in two, de-seed and slice. Rinse and pat dry the meat and cut into chunks.

4 Heat the oil in a pan and gently fry the onions. Add the meat.

5 Season the meat with salt and pepper. Add tomatoes, peppers and garlic. Pour the vegetable stock over and leave to draw for approx. 8 minutes.

6 Drain the rice. Drain the pineapple, pat dry and cut into small chunks.

7 Stir the rice and pineapples into the meat-vegetable mixture and season well with salt, pepper and chilli powder. Serve the rice casserole garnished with parsley leaves and red chillies.

■ **Serves 4**

250 g/9 oz wild rice

Salt

800 g/1 lb 12 oz tomatoes

1 onion

2 cloves garlic

2 red peppers

approx. 400 g/14 oz turkey breast

2 tbsp olive oil

Freshly ground pepper

200 ml/7 fl oz vegetable stock (cube)

1 tin pineapple (228 g/8 oz)

Chilli powder

Parsley and chillies for garnishing

Preparation time: approx. 30 minutes

Nutrition information per serving approx.: 31 g P, 13 g F, 57 g C, 507 kcal/2131 kJ

RICE WITH VEGETABLES AND PEPPERS

■ **Serves 4**

1 red onion

1 red pepper

2 cloves garlic

2 tbsp corn oil

200 g/7 oz long-grain rice

500 ml/17 fl oz vegetable stock (cube)

1 courgette

200 g/7 oz frozen peas

Salt

Freshly ground pepper

1/4 bunch coriander

1/4 bunch parsley

Preparation time: approx. 40 minutes

Nutrition information per serving approx.: 9 g P, 2 g F, 49 g C, 277 kcal/1163 kJ

1 Peel and slice the onion. Trim and rinse the pepper, halve, de-seed and cut into slices.

2 Peel and finely chop the garlic. Heat the oil in a saucepan and gently fry the onion, pepper and garlic.

3 Add the rice to the vegetables and fry gently. Pour over the vegetable stock and cook the rice over a low heat for approx. 18 minutes.

4 Trim and rinse the courgette, cut into slices and then fine sticks. Add the courgette and peas to the rice and simmer for another 5 minutes. Season thoroughly with salt and pepper.

5 Rinse and shake dry the herbs and mince them. Arrange the vegetable rice on plates and garnish with the herbs.

CORIANDER

Coriander is one of the most important herbs in Mexican cooking. It does not take heat very well and should always be added to the dishes shortly before the end of cooking time.

HERB OMELETTE WITH YOGHURT DRESSING

■ Serves 4

1 small courgette

100 g/3.5 oz whole fat yoghurt

150 g/2 oz crème fraîche

Salt

Freshly ground pepper

Chilli powder

4 eggs

100 ml/3 fl oz milk

1/2 bunch coriander

1/2 bunch parsley

1 red chilli

2 tbsp butter

150 g/5 oz grated cheddar

4 wheat flour tortillas

Preparation time: approx. 20 minutes

Nutrition information per serving approx.: 19 g P, 32 g F, 4 g C, 407 kcal/1709 kJ

1 Trim, rinse and then finely grate the courgette. Squeeze out the grated courgette in a colander. In a bowl, mix the yoghurt and crème fraîche. Add the grated courgette and season to a spicy taste with salt, pepper and chilli powder.

2 Beat the eggs with milk, salt and pepper. Rinse, shake dry and mince the herbs.

3 Trim and rinse the chilli, de-seed and finely chop. Stir the chilli and herbs into the beaten egg mixture.

4 Heat the butter in a frying pan and bake four omelettes, one after another. Shortly before the end of cooking time, sprinkle grated cheese over the omelettes.

5 Serve the omelettes garnished with the yoghurt dressing; they go well with wheat flour tortillas.

Fry the omelettes.

Serve garnished with yoghurt dressing.

HEARTY, FILLED CANNELLONI WITH TOMATO SAUCE

SUGGESTED DRINK

A Manhattan is a very suitable aperitif for this dish. Per serving, mix 2 tbsp whiskey with 3 tbsp red vermouth and season with a dash of lemon juice.

■ Serves 4

500 g/17 oz beef, from the shoulder

3 onions

2 cloves garlic

2 tbsp Masa (herb mixture available in specialist shops)

Salt

Freshly ground pepper

2 tbsp olive oil

Butter for the dish

16 Cannelloni

1 tin skinned tomatoes (480 g/16 oz)

2 red chillies

150 g/5 oz grated fresh Parmesan cheese

Preparation time: approx. 1 hour

Nutrition information per serving approx.: 45 g P, 20 g F, 23 g C, 492 kcal/2068 kJ

1 Rinse and pat dry the meat and cut into small chunks. Peel and finely chop the onions. Peel and crush the garlic.

2 Mix the meat with onions, garlic and herbs. Heat the oil in a frying pan and gently fry the meat.

3 Brush an ovenproof dish with butter. Preheat the oven to 200 °C/390 °F/ gas mark 6.

4 Fill the cannelloni with the meat paste and place into the dish. Drain the tomatoes, keeping the tomato juice in a bowl. Squash the tomatoes with a fork.

5 Spread the tomatoes and tomato juice over the cannelloni. Rinse and de-seed the chillies, finely chop and sprinkle them over the tomatoes. Top with cheese and cook in the centre of the oven for approx. 30 minutes.

BAKED FRUITY SWEET POTATOES

1 Rinse, peel and slice the potatoes. Boil in lightly salted water for approx. 10 minutes.

2 Brush an dish with butter. Preheat the oven to 180 °C/355 °F/gas mark 4.

3 Peel the pineapple, cut into four pieces, remove the inedible centre stalk and chop the fruit.

4 Drain the sliced sweet potatoes, place them in the ovenproof dish and spread over the pineapple chunks.

5 Mix the remaining ingredients and spread them over pineapple and potatoes. Cook in the centre of the oven for approx. 8 minutes.

Remove the centre stalk of the pineapple.

These baked sweet potatoes are especially good with spicy meat dishes.

■ **Serves 4**

4 large sweet potatoes

Salt

Butter for the dish

1 small pineapple or 300 g/10 oz tinned pineapple

Freshly ground pepper

Fresh grated nutmeg

2 tbsp fresh grated ginger

Cinnamon

3 tbsp rum

Preparation time: approx. 30 minutes

Nutrition information per serving approx.: 3 g P, 9 g F, 42 g C, 278 kcal/1167 kJ

WESTERN-STYLE HUEVOS RANCHEROS

Serves 4

450 g/1 lb
wheat flour

1 tbsp salt

1 tbsp bicarbonate
of soda

3 tbsp lard

1/2 tin skinned toma-
toes (480 g/16 oz)

4 red chillies

2 tbsp olive oil

1 clove garlic

1 tbsp wine vinegar

Salt

Freshly ground pepper

Caster sugar

3 tbsp butter

8 eggs

Preparation time:
approx. 50 minutes

Nutrition information
per serving approx.:
27 g P, 25 g F, 74 g C,
672 kcal/2824 kJ

1 Knead together the flour, salt, bicarbonate of soda and 1 tbsp lard. Stir in 180 ml/6 fl oz water.

2 Form the dough into 12 balls and roll out between two sheets of cling film into flat loaves of approx. 10 cm/4" Ø.

3 Heat the remaining lard in a frying pan and bake the loaves on both sides until the edges turn slightly brown and the loaves begin to rise. Keep the tortillas in a warm place.

4 Squash the tomatoes with a fork. Trim and rinse the chillies, de-seed and finely chop. Heat the olive oil in a saucepan and gently fry the tomatoes and chillies.

5 Peel the garlic and crush it into the tomato sauce. Add the vinegar and season to taste with salt, pepper and caster sugar.

6 Heat the butter in a frying pan and fry the eggs.

7 Place each egg on one tortilla and serve with the remaining tortillas and the tomato salsa.

Squash the tomatoes with a fork.   Finely chop the chillies.

Gently fry tomatoes and chillies.

Add the crushed garlic.

Fry the eggs.

MEAT AND POULTRY

Steaks, fricassees or grilled goodies:
on the following pages you will
discover a large variety of savoury
meat and poultry dishes.

PORK SHOULDER MEXICAN STYLE

■ Serves 4

800 g/1 lb 12 oz pork shoulder, bones removed

2 onions

2 cloves garlic

1/4 bunch coriander

1/4 bunch oregano

2 green peppers

3 tbsp butter

Salt

Freshly ground pepper

2 courgettes

1 red onion

2 tbsp olive oil

80 g/2.75 oz grated Cheddar cheese

Preparation time: approx. 30 minutes

Nutrition information per serving approx.: 37 g P, 73 g F, 5 g C, 892 kcal/3749 kJ

1 Rinse and pat dry the meat and cut into strips. Peel and coarsely chop the onions. Peel and finely chop the garlic.

2 Rinse and shake dry the herbs and pick off the leaves. Trim and rinse the peppers, slit open and de-seed, cut into slices.

3 Heat the butter in a pan. Gently fry the onions and peppers. Add meat, garlic and oregano. Fry the meat on all sides. Season with salt and pepper. Simmer for approx. 10 minutes. Towards the end, add the coriander.

4 Trim and rinse the courgettes and cut into slices. Peel the red onion and cut into rings. Heat the olive oil in another frying pan and gently fry courgettes and red onion. Season the vegetables with salt and pepper.

5 Arrange the meat and vegetables on plates and sprinkle with the grated cheese. This dish goes well with rice.

TEX-MEX-STYLE CHILLI CON CARNE

1 Peel the onion and cut into cubes. Peel and finely chop the garlic. Thoroughly season the minced meat with salt, pepper and chilli powder.

2 Rinse the chillies, cut in two, de-seed and finely chop. Heat the oil in a saucepan and gently fry the onion. Add the minced meat, garlic and chillies and stir-fry for approx. 8 minutes.

3 Rinse, shake dry and mince the coriander. Drain the beans and tomatoes. Add the tomatoes and beef stock to the meat and simmer over a low heat for approx. 1 hour.

4 Add the beans 15 minutes before the end of cooking time. At the very end, stir in the minced coriander.

5 Cut the white rolls into slices and serve with the chilli con carne.

■ *Chilli con carne is also very nice served in a halved bell pepper. This is especially suitable for garden parties and other festive occasions.*

■ **Serves 4**

1 onion

2 cloves garlic

500 g/17 oz minced beef

Salt

Freshly ground pepper

Chilli powder

2 red chillies

2 tbsp olive oil

1 bunch coriander

2 tins red kidney beans (225 g/8 oz each)

1 tin skinned tomatoes (225 g/8 oz)

500 ml/17 fl oz beef stock

2 large white rolls

Preparation time: approx. 1 1/2 hours

Nutrition information per serving approx.: 39 g P, 38 g F, 33 g C, 685 kcal/2877 kJ

TURKEY BREAST FILLETS WITH PUMPKIN SEEDS

■ Serves 4

800 g/1 lb 12 oz turkey breast fillet

Salt

Freshly ground pepper

Sweet paprika powder

1 onion

3 tomatoes

1 clove garlic

3 tbsp olive oil

100 g/3.5 oz pumpkin seeds plus a few more for garnishing

Parsley for garnishing

Preparation time: approx. 20 minutes

Nutrition information per serving approx.: 56 g P, 13 g F, 5 g C, 405 kcal/1702 kJ

1 Rinse and pat dry the meat, cut into slices approx. 1 cm (0.4") thick and season with salt, pepper and paprika powder.

2 Peel and chop the onions. Rinse the tomatoes, make a crosswise incision, dip them in simmering water, skin and then chop them. Peel and crush the garlic.

3 Heat oil in a frying pan, fry the meat for approx. 3 minutes on each side.

4 Remove the meat from the pan and keep in a warm place. Gently fry the onion and garlic in the stock left in the pan. Add tomatoes and pumpkin seeds and gently fry, stirring continually. Season well with salt and pepper.

5 Blend the sauce with an electric hand whisk. Arrange the turkey breast fillets and sauce on the plates and serve garnished with parsley and pumpkin seeds.

PUMPKIN SEEDS

Pumpkin seeds have a very high oil content, which is why they quickly go bad. Always keep them in an airtight container and store in the fridge.

■ *A spicy potato gratin is the perfect combination for turkey breast fillets with pumpkin seeds. Another delicious choice are the sweet potatoes described on p. 89.*

SPICY LAMB FILLETS WITH OLIVES

■ **Serves 4**

800 g/1 lb 12 oz lamb fillet

Salt

Freshly ground pepper

3 cloves garlic

1 red pepper

1 onion

4 tbsp olive oil

Fat for deep fat frying

2 tsp pickled peppercorns

1 tin tomatoes (225 g/8 oz)

30 g/1 oz black olives, stoned

1 dash Tabasco sauce

50 g/1.75 oz crème fraîche

600 g/1 lb 15 oz young potatoes

Paprika powder

Preparation time: approx. 40 minutes

Nutrition information per serving approx.: 44 g P, 28 g F, 28 g C, 594 kcal/2497 kJ

1 Rinse the lamb fillets, pat dry, cut into medallions and season with salt and pepper. Peel and crush the garlic and brush the lamb medallions with it.

2 Rinse the pepper, slice open, remove seeds and core and cut into rings. Peel and chop the onion. Heat the oil in a frying pan, gently fry the onion, add the lamb medallions and fry on both sides for approx. 2 minutes each side. Preheat the deep fat fryer to 180 °C/355 °F.

3 Remove the meat and keep in a warm place. Add the peppercorns and pepper rings to the stock, drain the tomatoes and add these to the stock, as well as the olives. Pour 100 ml/3 fl oz water over and simmer for approx. 20 minutes. Season the sauce with salt, pepper and Tabasco sauce. Stir in the crème fraîche.

4 While the sauce is simmering, scrub the potatoes and cut them into thin slices, then fry them in the deep fat fryer until they are golden brown. Before serving, season the potatoes with salt and pepper.

5 Arrange the lamb medallions, sauce and country fries on plates.

Brush with garlic.

Fry the lamb fillets.

PORK FRICASSEE "PICADILLO"

SUGGESTED DRINK

A Limara is made by mixing 20 ml/scant 1 oz passion fruit juice, 40 ml/1.5 fl oz orange juice, 10 ml/.5 fl oz lemon juice and 100 ml/3 fl oz chilled mineral water. Serve the drink garnished with an orange slice.

■ **Serves 4**

800 g/1 lb 12 oz lean pork

Salt

Freshly ground pepper

Chilli powder

1 onion

2 cloves garlic

1 beef tomato

2 red peppers

2 tbsp olive oil

1/4 bunch coriander

1/4 bunch parsley

50 g/1.75 oz puréed tomato (in a pack)

Preparation time: approx. 45 minutes

Nutrition information per serving approx.: 38 g P, 31 g F, 3 g C, 488 kcal/2049 kJ

1 Rinse and pat dry the meat and cut into strips, then season with salt, pepper and chilli powder.

2 Peel and chop the onion. Peel and finely chop the garlic. Rinse the tomato, make a crosswise incision, dip in simmering water, skin and chop.

3 Trim and rinse the peppers, cut in two, de-seed and cut into slices.

4 Heat the oil in a frying pan. Gently fry the onion and garlic. Add the meat and peppers and stir-fry for approx. 5 minutes.

5 Rinse and shake dry the herbs, mince and add herbs and chopped tomatoes to the meat. Stir in the tomato purée and season once more with the spices.

6 Arrange the meat on plates. This dish goes well with rice.

SWEAT AND SOUR CHICKEN

1 Rinse and pat dry the meat, cut into chunks and season with salt and pepper. Crush the chillies in a mortar and remove the seeds.

2 Heat the oil in a frying pan and fry the meat. Add the chillies, stir in the sesame seeds.

3 Pour over the white wine and simmer for approx. 5 minutes. Drain the pineapple slices and cut them into cubes. Peel and slice the banana.

4 Add the pineapple and banana to the meat and season with salt and pepper.

5 Stir the starch in water and add to the meat. Season to taste with soy sauce. Arrange on plates.

Slice the banana.

■ **Serves 4**
850 g/1 lb 14 oz chicken breast fillet

Salt

Freshly ground pepper

2 dried chillies

2 tbsp olive oil

1 tbsp sesame seeds

125 ml/4 fl oz white wine

4 slices pineapple (tin)

1 banana

1 tbsp starch

2 tbsp soy sauce

Preparation time: approx. 40 minutes

Nutrition information per serving approx.: 50 g P, 12 g F, 15 g C, 427 kcal/1793 kJ

STUFFED BABY TURKEY IN WHITE WINE STOCK

■ **Serves 4**

20 g/2.5 oz chopped almonds

1 red pepper

1 green pepper

3 onions

1 clove garlic

3 tomatoes

1 apple

3 tbsp lemon juice

250 g/9 oz mixed minced meat

Salt

Freshly ground pepper

6 tbsp olive oil

50 g/1.75 oz sultanas

1 baby turkey, ready for cooking

200 ml/7 fl oz white wine

150 ml/5 fl oz vegetable stock

2 tbsp starch

2 tbsp crème fraîche

Preparation time: approx. 1 3/4 hours

Nutrition information per serving approx.: 65 g P, 37 g F, 12 g C, 705 kcal/2962 kJ

1 Roast the chopped almonds in a pan without any fat. Rinse the peppers, slice open, de-seed and cut into slices.

2 Peel and chop the onion. Peel the garlic and cut into slices. Trim and rinse the tomatoes and cut into slices. Peel the apple, remove the pips and core, chop and sprinkle with lemon juice.

3 In a bowl, knead the minced meat with salt and pepper. Heat 3 tbsp oil in a frying pan. Gently fry onions and garlic. Add the minced meat. Stir in the tomatoes, apple and sultanas, then the almonds and peppers. Season with salt and pepper. Preheat the oven to 180 °C/355 °F/gas mark 4.

4 Rinse the turkey under running water from the inside and outside and pat dry with a tea towel. Stuff with the minced meat mixture, tie up with wooden picks or kitchen thread.

5 Heat the remaining oil in a roasting pan and fry the turkey on all sides. Pour over the white wine and vegetable stock and cook in the centre of the oven for approx. 1 hour. Pour the stock over the turkey regularly.

6 Remove the turkey from the roasting pan, bring the stock to the boil and add starch and crème fraîche. Season with salt and pepper. Carve the turkey and serve with stuffing and gravy.

Roast the chopped almonds.

Chop the apple ...

... and sprinkle with lemon juice.

Fry the minced meat.

Stir in the apples and sultanas.

DRUMSTICKS IN A FRUITY SAUCE

Serves 4

**12 drumsticks
(lower part of a
chicken thigh, order
at your butcher's)**

4 cloves garlic

1 onion

1/4 tsp cinnamon

1/4 tsp ground clover

1/4 tsp ground saffron

3 tbsp olive oil

3 tbsp sultanas

**125 ml/4 fl oz
chicken stock**

**1 medium-sized
pineapple**

70 ml/2.5 fl oz sherry

Preparation time:
approx. 50 minutes

Nutrition information
per serving approx.:
34 g P, 39 g F, 12 g C,
582 kcal/2446 kJ

1 Rinse and pat dry the drumsticks. Peel and crush the garlic. Peel and finely chop the onion. Mix cinnamon, clover and saffron and rub the drumsticks with this mixture.

2 Heat the oil in a frying pan and fry the drumsticks together with the onion and garlic. Add the sultanas and pour the chicken stock over. Bring to the boil and then simmer over a low heat for approx. 40 minutes.

3 In the meantime, peel the pineapple, remove the centre stalk and cut the flesh into medium-sized cubes.

4 Add pineapple and sherry approx. 10 minutes before the end of cooking time.

BEEF CUTLETS "BIG MAN"

1 Rinse and pat dry the cutlets and season with salt and pepper. Give the flour into a bowl. Beat 1/2 l/17 fl oz of the milk with the tequila and eggs.

2 Turn the cutlets in the flour, then dip them in the egg-milk mix and turn them in the flour once more.

3 Heat the oil in a frying pan and fry the cutlets until both sides have turned golden brown. Remove them from the pan and keep warm.

4 Pour 4 tbsp of the egg-milk mix into the pan and heat up. Stir in 1/4 ml/ 9 fl oz milk and simmer until the sauce begins to set.

5 Stir in the peppercorns and season to taste with salt, pepper and chilli powder.

6 Arrange the cutlets with the sauce. This dish goes well with black beans.

■ **Serves 4**

4 beef cutlets

Salt

Freshly ground pepper

375 g/13 oz maize flour

750 ml/1 pint 7 fl oz milk

2 cl/1/2 tsp tequila

2 eggs

3 tbsp peanut oil

2 tbsp green peppercorns

Chilli powder

Preparation time: approx. 30 minutes

Nutrition information per serving approx.: 47 g P, 17 g F, 21 g C, 475 kcal/1998 kJ

POULTRY WRAPS YUCATAN STYLE

■ **Serves 4**

4 cloves garlic

1/4 tsp turmeric

1/4 tsp chopped oregano

125 ml/4 fl oz orange juice

A dash of Tabasco sauce

12 chicken wings

Salt

Freshly ground black pepper

2 onions

4 beef tomatoes

6 medium large banana leaves

4 tbsp corn oil

Preparation time: approx. 1 hour

Time for marinating: approx. 3 hours

Nutrition information per serving approx.: 26 g P, 29 g F, 7 g C, 427 kcal/1793 kJ

1 Peel and crush the garlic, then mix it with turmeric, oregano, orange juice and a generous dash of Tabasco sauce. Rinse the chicken wings and marinate them in the paste for approx. 3 hours.

2 Remove the meat from the marinade, pat dry and season with salt and pepper. Preheat the oven to 160 °C/ 320 °F/gas mark 2/3.

3 Peel and chop the onions. Peel, trim and cube the tomatoes. Rinse and pat dry the banana leaves, cut them in half and spread them on the work surface.

4 Place one chicken wing on each leaf and spread some tomato and onions over.

5 Brush the ingredients with some oil. Wrap the banana leaves into small parcels and brush with oil. Cook in the centre of the oven for approx. 40 minutes.

■ *The chicken wraps can also be prepared in dried maize leaves. The maize leaves are soaked in cold water for approx. 1 hour, after which you can pat them dry and then proceed as with the banana leaves.*

CHICKEN TEXICANA WITH CHILLI

Serves 4

Dried chillies to taste

4 chicken thighs, each approx. 200 g/7 oz

Salt

Freshly ground pepper

2 tbsp sunflower oil

2 red bell peppers

1 yellow bell pepper

1 green bell pepper

150 g/5 oz sweet corn (tinned)

200 ml/7 fl oz chilli sauce (ready-made)

Preparation time: approx. 40 minutes

Nutrition information per serving approx.: 39 g P, 43 g F, 26 g C, 703 kcal/2952 kJ

1 Grind the chillies in a mortar, remove the seeds.

2 Rinse and pat dry the meat and season with salt, pepper and chilli powder.

3 Heat the oil in a frying pan and fry the meat on all sides until golden brown. In the meantime, trim and rinse the bell peppers and chop them. Drain the sweet corn.

4 Add the bell peppers and sweet corn to the meat. Pour the chilli sauce over, cover and leave to simmer over a low heat for approx. 20 minutes.

5 Arrange the chicken thighs and salsa on plates and serve with baguette or tacos.

Fry the chicken thighs.

Add the chopped bell peppers.

FISH AND SEAFOOD

The delicacies caught in rivers, lakes and the Pacific Ocean combine beautifully with the savoury ingredients of Tex-Mex cooking.

SOLE FILLETS "VERACRUZ" IN VEGETABLE SAUCE

SUGGESTED DRINK

As an aperitif, prepare a Trocadero by mixing 20 ml/ scant 1 fl oz dry vermouth, 40 ml/1.5 fl oz grenadine and 30 ml/1 fl oz orange juice. Serve the drink in a cocktail glass, garnished with a cocktail cherry.

■ **Serves 4**

1 onion

2 cloves garlic

2 beef tomatoes

2 green peppers

3 tbsp olive oil

150 ml/5 fl oz vegetable stock (cube)

Salt

Freshly ground pepper

4 sole fillets

3 tbsp lemon juice

Butter for the dish

80 g/2.75 green olives

Preparation time: approx. 45 minutes

Nutrition information per serving approx.: 35 g P, 12 g F, 2 g C, 299 kcal/1255 kJ

1 Peel and chop the onions. Peel and finely chop the garlic.

2 Rinse and chop the tomatoes. Trim and rinse the peppers and cut into rings.

3 Heat the oil in a saucepan, gently fry onion, garlic and peppers. Add the tomatoes and pour the stock over, then season with salt and pepper.

4 Preheat the oven to 180 °C/355 °F/ gas mark 4. Sprinkle the fish with lemon juice. Brush an ovenproof dish with butter and place the fish in it. Spread the vegetable sauce over the fish and cover the dish with tin foil.

5 Cook in the centre of the oven for approx. 20 minutes. Before serving, garnish with the olives.

MARINATED TURBOT WITH VEGETABLES

1 Cut the fish into strips and place in a saucepan. Pour over lemon juice until the fish is entirely covered by the juice.

2 Leave the fish to draw in the lemon juice for approx. 8 minutes over a very low heat.

3 Peel the onions and cut into rings. Trim and rinse the tomato, then chop it. Trim and rinse the peppers, cut in two, de-seed and cut into rings.

4 Rinse and shake dry the herbs and finely mince them. Remove the fish pan from the heat. Add the herbs, onion, peppers and tomatoes. Season with salt and pepper. Stir in Tabasco and Worcestershire sauce.

5 Place the fish in the fridge and let it draw in the marinade for approx. 8 hours. Serve with baguette.

Place the fish in a saucepan.

■ **Serves 4**

800 g/1 lb 12 oz turbot fillets

60 ml/2 fl oz lemon juice

2 red onions

1 large tomato

2 green peppers

1/4 bunch coriander

1/4 bunch parsley

Salt, freshly ground pepper

1 dash Tabasco sauce

1 dash Worcestershire sauce

Preparation time: approx. 40 minutes
Time for marinating: approx. 8 hours

Nutrition information per serving approx.:
34 g P, 4 g F, 2 g C,
206 kcal/867 kJ

SPICY PRAWNS "FUEGO"

1 Rinse the tomatoes, make a crosswise incision, dip them in simmering water, bathe in cold water, skin and chop them.

2 Peel and crush the garlic. Peel the onions and cut into rings.

3 Rinse and pat dry the prawns. Heat the butter in a frying pan and gently fry onions and garlic. Add the chopped tomatoes and simmer for approx. 5 minutes. Add the prawns.

4 Stir in the chilli sauce and season to taste with a little salt and pepper. Serve the spicy prawns garnished with herbs.

Make a crosswise incision into the tomatoes.

Dip them in simmering water.

Wait until the skin begins to come off.

Remove the skin.

Chop the tomatoes.

Add the prawns.

TUNA STEAKS AND SHRIMPS IN CHILLI DRESSING

■ Serves 4

50 ml/2 fl oz lemon juice

4 tuna steaks

100 ml/3 fl oz orange juice

2 shallots

2 red chillies

2 tbsp olive oil

1/2 bunch parsley

Salt

Freshly ground pepper

100 g/3.5 oz pre-cooked shrimps

Preparation time: approx. 20 minutes

Time for marinating: approx. 3 hours

Nutrition information per serving approx.: 49 g P, 38 g F, 6 g C, 623 kcal/2618 kJ

1 Bring approx. 1 l/1 quart water to the boil with some of the lemon juice and draw the tuna steaks in it for approx. 4 minutes.

2 Remove the fish steaks and pat dry. Mix the remaining lemon juice with the orange juice and marinate the tuna steaks in this for approx. 3 hours.

3 Peel the shallots and cut into rings. Trim and rinse the chillies, cut in halves, de-seed and finely chop. Mix the shallots and chillies with the olive oil. Rinse and shake dry the parsley, mince and add to the paste. Season with salt and pepper.

4 Remove the steaks from the marinade, pat dry and arrange on plates together with the shrimps. Spoon over the chilli dressing.

DEEP FRIED SCALLOPS WITH SPICY SALSA

1 Rinse and pat dry the scallops. Rinse the chillies, slice open, de-seed and finely chop them. Peel and chop the onions.

2 Mix the milk with flour and Tabasco sauce. Stir in the onions and chillies. Season to taste with salt, pepper and chilli powder.

3 Rinse and dry the parsley, mince and add to the dough.

4 Heat the oil in a deep fat fryer. Turn the scallops in the dough and fry in the deep fat fryer until they are golden brown.

5 Arrange the fried scallops on plates and add a spoonful of the spicy chilli salsa. Serve garnished with lime slices and herbs.

■ **Serves 4**

800 g/1 lb 12 oz scallops (defrosted)

2 red chillies

2 onions

125 ml/4 fl oz milk

125 g/4.5 oz flour

1 dash Tabasco sauce

Salt

Freshly ground pepper

Chilli powder

1/2 bunch parsley

Oil for deep fat frying

120 ml/4 fl oz chilli sauce

Lime slices and herbs for garnishing

Preparation time: approx. 20 minutes

Nutrition information per serving approx.: 29 g P, 19 g F, 37 g C, 475 kcal/1997 kJ

ROCK LOBSTER TAILS IN RED SAUCE

■ Serves 4

2 rock lobster tails (frozen)

2 tbsp butter

2 red chillies

Salt

Freshly ground pepper

Paprika powder

1 dash Tabasco sauce

200 ml/7 fl oz white wine

1 onion

1 clove garlic

1 dash Worcestershire sauce

100 g/3.5 oz ketchup

Some lime juice

2 tbsp crème fraîche

Dill for garnishing

Lime peel for garnishing

Preparation time: approx. 30 minutes

Nutrition information per serving approx.: 38 g P, 6 g F, 10 g C, 274 kcal/1152 kJ

1 Rinse and pat dry the rock lobster tails. Heat the butter in a frying pan and thoroughly fry the rock lobster tails on all sides.

2 Trim and rinse the chillies, slice open, de-seed and mince. Add them to the rock lobsters and season with salt, pepper, paprika powder and some Tabasco sauce.

3 Pour the white wine over and simmer the rock lobsters in this stock for approx. 15 minutes, over a low heat.

4 Peel and chop the onion. Peel and crush the garlic. Mix the Worcestershire sauce and ketchup, then add the onion and garlic.

5 Stir in the lime juice and crème fraîche. Season with salt, pepper and paprika powder.

6 Arrange the rock lobster tails on plates, spoon over the sauce and serve garnished with dill and lime slices.

ROCK LOBSTERS

The tail of a rock lobster is the animal's part with the most savoury flesh. As a frozen product, they are available in every well-stocked supermarket.

TEQUILA PRAWNS IN A CHEESE CRUST

■ **Serves 4**

16 king prawns with tails

250 g/9 oz cheese spread with herbs

2 tbsp tequila

5 tbsp white wine

1 onion

2 cloves garlic

Salt

Freshly ground pepper

Paprika powder

Oil for deep fat frying

100 g/3.5 oz breadcrumbs

Herbs for garnishing

Preparation time: approx. 30 minutes

Nutrition information per serving approx.:
50 g P, 16 g F, 26 g C, 504 kcal/2116 kJ

1 Trim, rinse and pat dry the prawns. Squash the cheese spread with a fork and stir in the tequila and white wine.

2 Peel and chop the onion. Peel and crush the garlic. Stir into the cheese sauce and season with salt, pepper and paprika powder.

3 Heat the oil in the deep fat fryer. Pour the breadcrumbs onto a plate, turn the prawns in the breadcrumbs, then bathe the prawns in the cheese sauce.

4 Fry the prawns in the deep fat fryer until they are golden brown. Serve garnished with herbs. These prawns go well with nachos and a yoghurt dip.

Turn the prawns in the breadcrumbs.

Bathe in the cheese sauce.

GRILLED KING PRAWNS WITH MUSTARD DRESSING

SUGGESTED DRINK

For a Green Witch, stir 50 ml/2 fl oz pineapple juice with 30 ml/1 fl oz pear juice, 20 ml/scant 1 oz lemon juice and 20 ml/scant 1 oz Blue Curaçao. Fill up the long drink glasses with ice cubes and serve garnished with an orange slice.

■ Serves 4

12 king prawns, not peeled

3 cloves garlic

4 tbsp olive oil

Salt

Freshly ground pepper

80 ml/2.5 fl oz white wine

30 g/1 oz Dijon mustard

100 g/3.5 oz mayonnaise

1 dash Worcestershire sauce

1 dash Tabasco sauce

2 tbsp cream

Dill and lime slices for garnishing

Preparation time: approx. 20 minutes

Nutrition information per serving approx.: 16 g P, 21 g F, 4 g C, 309 kcal/1298 kJ

1 Rinse and pat dry the king prawns. Peel and crush the garlic and stir with the olive oil. Season with salt and pepper.

2 Brush the king prawns with the garlic oil and cook them on the grill for approx. 10 minutes.

3 In the meantime, beat the white wine, mustard, mayonnaise, Worcestershire sauce, Tabasco sauce and cream together and season with salt and pepper.

4 Serve the king prawns and mustard dressing and garnish each plate with dill and lime slices.

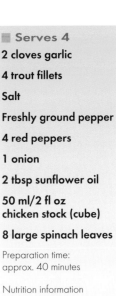

PUNGENT TROUT FILLETS FROM THE OVEN

1 Peel and crush the garlic and brush the fish with it. Season with salt and pepper.

2 Trim and rinse the peppers, slice open, de-seed and cut into rings. Peel the onion and cut it into rings.

3 Heat the oil in a frying pan and gently fry the onion and peppers. Season with salt and pepper. Pour the chicken stock over. Preheat the oven to 180 °C/355 °F/ gas mark 4.

4 Rinse and pat dry the spinach leaves and place two spinach leaves next to another, one slightly covering the edge of the other, on the work surface.

5 Lay the fillets on the spinach leaves and spread the vegetable mixture over the fish. Wrap the spinach leaves around the fish and then wrap them up in tin foil. Cook the trout fillets in the centre of the preheated oven for approx. 20 minutes.

Wrap the fish up in the spinach.

■ Serves 4

2 cloves garlic

4 trout fillets

Salt

Freshly ground pepper

4 red peppers

1 onion

2 tbsp sunflower oil

50 ml/2 fl oz chicken stock (cube)

8 large spinach leaves

Preparation time: approx. 40 minutes

Nutrition information per serving approx.: 27 g P, 51 g F, 4 g C, 624 kcal/2620 kJ

CEVICHE OF FRESH GILTHEAD FILLETS

■ **Serves 4**

4 very fresh gilthead fillets

3 tbsp lemon juice

2 onions

3 tomatoes

4 red chillies

1/2 bunch coriander

1/2 bunch parsley

5 limes

Salt

Freshly ground pepper

200 g/7 oz tortillas

Preparation time: approx. 20 minutes

Standing time: approx. 1 hour

Nutrition information per serving approx.: 36 g P, 1 g F, 2 g C, 189 kcal/794 kJ

1 Sprinkle the fillets with lemon juice and cut into chunks.

2 Peel the onions and cut into rings. Trim and rinse the tomatoes and chop them. Trim and rinse the chillies, slice open, de-seed and finely chop them. Rinse, shake dry and mince the herbs.

3 Squeeze out the juice of the limes and mix the lime juice with the chopped tomatoes, onions, chillies and herbs. Season with salt and pepper. Add the fish chunks and leave to draw at room temperature for approx. 1 hour. Stir again and again to make sure that the fish is always covered in juice.

4 Keep in the refrigerator until the fish is served; do not keep the fish for longer than 24 hours. Serve with tortillas.

Cut the fish into chunks.

Chop the tomatoes.

Squeeze the juice out of the limes.

Stir in the herbs.

Add the fish chunks.

CAKES AND DESSERTS

The typical Mexican desserts
such as bakes and egg dishes
have a long tradition. Even today,
these delicious dishes are favourites
of Tex-Mex cooking.

MAIZE MUFFINS IN A CERAMIC BOWL

■ Serves 4

200 g/7 oz flour

200 g/7 oz maize flour

4 tsp caster sugar

1 tsp baking powder

2 eggs

1 tsp salt

125 ml/4.5 fl oz milk

100 g/3.5 oz soft, unsalted butter

Butter for the dish

Preparation time: approx. 40 minutes

Standing time: approx. 30 minutes

Nutrition information per serving approx.: 14 g P, 6 g F, 71 g C, 427 kcal/1795 kJ

1 Mix the flour, maize flour, caster sugar and baking powder.

2 Beat the eggs in a bowl with the salt, then add the milk and butter. Mix with the flour, cover the dough and leave to rest for approx. 30 minutes.

3 Preheat the oven to 180 °C/355 °F/ gas mark 4. Line 12 small ceramic bowls with greaseproof paper and fill in the dough.

4 Bake the dough in the centre of the oven for approx. 20 minutes, until the muffins take on a light golden hue.

5 Remove the muffins and greaseproof paper from the bowls, pull off the paper and serve the muffins on a tray or large plate.

MAIZE FLOUR

Maize flour is made by thoroughly grinding maize kernels and is used very much in Mexican cooking.

■ *In America, muffins are usually baked in special muffin trays. However, there is no need to buy this specifically since they turn out just as well if baked in the above-mentioned ovenproof bowls.*

MEXICAN FLAN

■ Serves 4

**200 g/7 oz
caster sugar**

**1 1/2 l/1 quart 13 fl oz
milk**

2 tbsp caster sugar

5 eggs

5 egg yolks

1 tsp custard powder

Preparation time:
approx. 40 minutes

Nutrition information
per serving approx.:
27 g P, 31 g F, 64 g C,
690 kcal/2899 kJ

1 In a saucepan, heat the sugar and 2 tbsp water over a medium heat and stir until the sugar begins to melt. Increase the heat and keep stirring until the caramel has turned a light brown.

2 Immediately pour the caramel into 4 flan dishes (each holding approx. 100 ml/3 fl oz) and swivel them until their bottoms are covered in caramel. Preheat the oven to 150 °C/300 °F/gas mark 2.

3 In a bowl, beat the milk with 2 tbsp sugar, eggs and custard powder and then pour the mixture into the flan dishes.

4 Cook in a *bain-marie* in the centre of the oven for approx. 1 1/4 hours.

5 Leave the flans to cool a little. Go along the edge of the flan dishes with a thin knife to loosen the pudding from the dish, then turn the flans onto dessert plates.

Even out the caramel.

Pour the egg mixture into the flan dishes.

TRADITIONAL MAIZE LOAF

SUGGESTED DRINK

For a hot chocolate,
heat up 150 ml/5 fl oz milk,
50 ml/2 fl oz cream,
1 tbsp caster sugar and
50 g/1.75 oz dark chocolate
in a saucepan, stirring
continually.

■ **Serves 4**

250 ml/9 fl oz milk

4 tbsp butter

2 eggs

**400 g/14 oz
wheat flour**

175 g/6 oz maize flour

1/2 tsp salt

1 tsp caster sugar

1 tbsp baking powder

Preparation time:
approx. 45 minutes

Nutrition information
per serving approx.:
20 g P, 24 g F, 106 g C,
767 kcal/3224 kJ

1 Preheat the oven to 200 °C/390 °F/ gas mark 6. Warm up the milk and melt the butter in a saucepan. Beat the eggs in a bowl.

2 Give the flour, maize flour, salt, sugar and baking powder into a bowl and mix.

3 Add milk, butter and eggs to the flour and knead to a smooth dough. Form the dough into a long roll, turning the two ends in the opposite direction.

4 Bake in the centre of the oven for approx. 20 minutes.

■ *A good accompaniment to a maize loaf is a mixed salad with a spicy dressing.*

SWEET PEANUT COOKIES WITH CUSTARD

1 Crush the peanuts with a mortar, then knead them thoroughly with butter, flour, syrup and caster sugar.

2 Preheat the oven to 180 °C/355 °F/ gas mark 4. Form the dough into balls of approx. 2 cm/0.8" Ø.

3 Line a baking tray with greaseproof paper and spread the balls on it, making sure the distance between them is large enough.

4 Bake in the centre of the oven for approx. 12 minutes, until the balls have taken the shape of large, flat coins. Prepare the custard as advised on the package and serve with the peanut cookies.

Form the dough into balls.

■ **Serves 4**

50 g/1.75 oz peanuts, unsalted

50 g/1.75 oz unsalted butter

50 g/1.75 oz flour

50 g/1.75 oz maple syrup

40 g/1.5 oz caster sugar

1 portion custard

Preparation time: approx. 40 minutes

Nutrition information per serving approx.: 4 g P, 16 g F, 28 g C, 289 kcal/1216 kJ

BREAD PUDDING WITH APPLES AND SYRUP

Serves 4

150 g/5 oz
brown sugar

1 tbsp honey

1 cinnamon stick

2 clovers

1 wedge organic
orange peel

4 dry rolls

40 g/1.5 oz
unsalted butter

2 apples

Butter for the dish

250 g/9 oz full fat
cream cheese

150 g/5 oz sultanas

75 g/2.5 oz
chopped walnuts

75 g/2.5 oz
chopped almonds

Preparation time:
approx. 50 minutes

Nutrition information
per serving approx.:
15 g P, 34 g F, 81 g C,
728 kcal/3057 kJ

1 Heat 250 ml/9 oz water in a saucepan. Add sugar, honey and the spices. Cook until it has turned into a thin syrup. Remove the spices and leave the syrup to cool.

2 Cut the rolls into cubes. Heat the butter in a frying pan and roast the bread cubes in it.

3 Rinse, peel and slice the apples. Brush an ovenproof dish with butter.

4 Spoon half of the cream cheese, the apples, sultanas and nuts into the dish. Pour half of the syrup over. Preheat the oven to 180 °C/355 °F/gas mark 4.

5 In layers, add the bread cubes, then the remaining half of the cream cheese, the remaining sultanas and nuts. Top with the remaining apples and pour the rest of the cinnamon syrup over.

6 Cover the dish with tin foil and bake in the centre of the oven for approx. 20 minutes.

Slice the apples.

Brush the dish with butter.

Add a layer of apples.

Pour the syrup over the ingredients.

Cover the pudding with apple slices.

MEXICAN-STYLE CAJETA

■ Serves 4

11/2 l/1 quart 13 fl oz milk

1 tsp maize starch

1 pinch baking powder

1 vanilla pod

500 g/17 oz light cane sugar

Chocolate chips

Wafer rolls

Preparation time: approx. 20 minutes

Nutrition information per serving approx.: 12 g P, 13 g F, 142 g C, 739 kcal/3103 kJ

1 Heat the milk in a flat saucepan. Add the maize starch and baking powder.

2 Scratch the vanilla mark out of the pod and stir into the milk; add the cane sugar.

3 Stir continually over a low heat until the sugar has dissolved.

4 Bring the mixture to the boil and then add the baking powder-starch mix. Keep simmering over a low heat until the liquid begins to thicken.

5 Fill into mugs and sprinkle with chocolate chips. Serve the Cajeta with wafer rolls.

RICE PUDDING WITH PINE NUTS

1 Bring the rice to the boil in approx. 2 1/2 quarts lightly salted water, with the cinnamon stick.

2 Heat the milk in a saucepan. Whisk the egg yolks with the sugar and vanilla mark scraped from the pod. Slowly stir the hot milk into this mixture.

3 Roast the pine nuts in a fat-free frying pan. Fork the egg milk, currants and pine nuts into the rice.

4 Simmer over a low heat until the rice is cooked with a little bite to it. Remove the cinnamon stick.

5 Arrange the rice pudding on plates and sprinkle with the ground cinnamon and sugar.

■ *This favourite dessert can be eaten both warm, lukewarm and cold. If you prepare it with long-grain rice instead of rice pudding rice, it will have more bite to it.*

■ **Serves 4**

200 g/7 oz long-grain rice

Salt

1 cinnamon stick

500 ml/17 fl oz milk

2 egg yolks

7 tbsp caster sugar

1 vanilla pod

4 tbsp pine nuts

50 g/1.75 oz currants

Ground cinnamon and sugar for sprinkling over

Preparation time: approx. 30 minutes

Nutrition information per serving approx.: 13 g P, 15 g F, 56 g C, 472 kcal/1983 kJ

MEXICAN-STYLE BUNUELOS

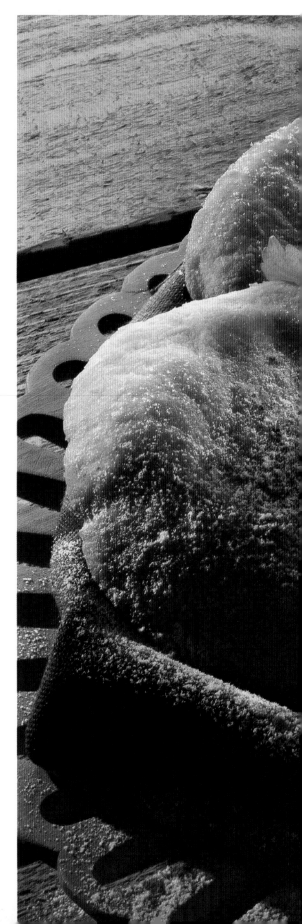

■ Serves 4

200 g/7 oz flour

1/2 tsp baking powder

1 tbsp cane sugar

11 pinch salt

80 g/2.75 oz butter

1 egg

5–6 tbsp milk

Oil for deep fat frying

100 g/3.5 oz icing sugar

1 tsp ground cinnamon

Preparation time: approx. 30 minutes

Standing time: approx. 30 minutes

Nutrition information per serving approx.: 5 g P, 38 g F, 62 g C, 633 kcal/2659 kJ

1 Sieve the flour into a bowl, add baking powder, sugar and salt.

2 Knead the butter into the flour mixture. Beat the egg with the milk and pour it into the butter-flour mixture. Knead to make a firm dough and leave to rest for approx. 30 minutes.

3 Preheat the oil in your deep fat fryer to 170 °C/340 °F. Take walnut-size pieces from the dough and form them into balls. Dust your work surface with flour and thinly roll out the balls.

4 Bake the fritters in the deep fat fryer; the Bunuelos will puff up slightly. Lay them out on absorbent kitchen paper. Mix ground cinnamon and icing sugar and sprinkle over the Bunuelos.

■ *Traditionally, Bunuelos were fried in lard. But in the recent decades, the trend has changed to frying them in vegetable oil.*

BUNUELOS

Bunuelos are traditionally eaten in the festive season, mostly at Christmas. Instead of serving them with cinnamon and sugar, they also taste delicious dipped in maple syrup.

LIME CAKE WITH MERINGUE

Serves 4

150 g/5 oz flour

1 tbsp icing sugar

125 g/4.5 oz butter

Butter for the baking tray

Lentils for pre-baking

6 eggs, yolks and whites separated

400 ml/14 fl oz tinned milk

5 limes

175 g/6 oz caster sugar

1/4 tsp baking powder

Preparation time: approx. 1 hour

Standing time: approx. 1 hour

Nutrition information per serving approx.: 18 g P, 40 g F, 73 g C, 756 kcal/3178 kJ

1 Quickly knead the flour, icing sugar, 100 ml/3 fl oz water and flaked butter into a smooth dough. Form into a ball, wrap in cling film and leave to rest in the fridge for approx. 1 hour.

2 Preheat the oven to 200 °C/390 °F/ gas mark 6. Brush a baking tray of approx. 25 cm/10" Ø with butter. Roll out the dough between two sheets of cling film until it is about 28 cm/ 11" in Ø and then lay it into the baking tray, without the cling film. Press the pastry around the edges.

3 Pinch the bottom of the pastry with your fork several times, line it with greaseproof paper, pour the lentils over and pre-bake it in the centre of the oven for approx. 15 minutes.

4 Remove the lentils and bake the pastry for another 15 minutes. Then leave to cool.

5 Whisk the egg yolks with the tinned milk until it gets creamy. Wash the limes in hot water, pat dry and finely grate the peel of two limes. Squeeze out the juice, measure out 125 ml/4 fl oz of the juice and stir into the egg cream; also add the grated lime peel.

6 Pour the cream over the pastry and even out. Whisk the egg whites, sugar and baking powder and spread over the cream. Bake in the lower part of the oven for approx. 15 minutes, until the meringue turns golden brown.

Lay the pastry in the baking tray.

Press around the edges.

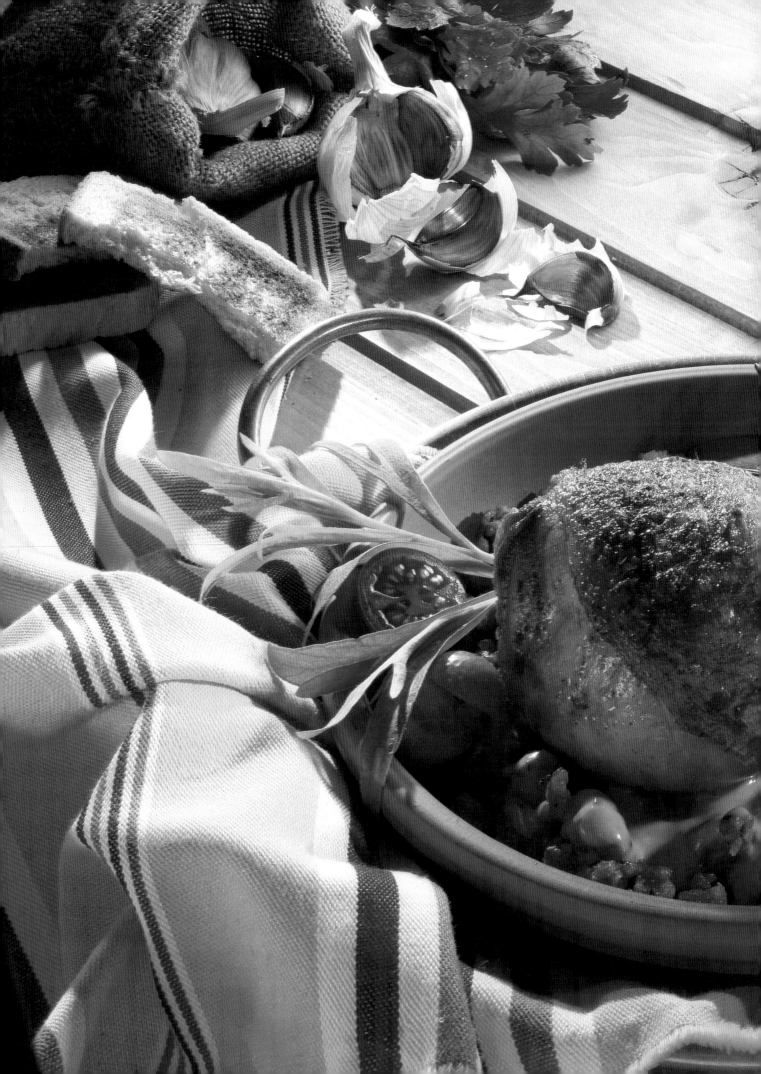

Classics from American Cooking

Here you will find the favourite specialities from all across the American continent: be it pumpkin soup and turkey, or hamburgers and apple pie.

THANKSGIVING PUMPKIN SOUP IN PUMPKIN HALVES

SUGGESTED DRINK

Mexican Power: per portion, mix 50 ml/2 fl oz apple juice with 30 ml/1 fl oz grenadine and 20 ml/scant 1 oz lemon juice and season to taste with a little almond syrup. Garnish with miniature apples.

■ Serves 4

2 small garden pumpkins

50 g/1.75 oz butter

1 tbsp caster sugar

3/4 l/1 pint 7 fl oz milk

1/2 tsp ground mace

Freshly ground nutmeg

1/2 tsp ground clover

Salt

Freshly ground pepper

Herbs for garnishing

Preparation time: approx. 40 minutes

Nutrition information per serving approx.: 4 g P, 11 g F, 19 g C, 203 kcal/852 kJ

1 Cut the pumpkins in halves, remove the seeds and stringy bits, scrape out the flesh with a spoon, leaving an edge of approx. 0.5 cm/0.2".

2 Heat the butter in a saucepan, stir in the pumpkin chunks and gently cook over a low heat.

3 Add the sugar. Slowly stir in the milk.

4 Thoroughly season to taste with mace, nutmeg, ground clover, salt and pepper.

5 Leave the soup to simmer for approx. 20 minutes and then blend with your electric hand whisk.

6 Spoon the pumpkin soup into the pumpkin halves and serve garnished with herbs and freshly ground pepper.

SEAFOOD SOUP WITH OKRA PODS

1 Peel the onions and cut into rings. Rinse and chop the tomatoes, trim, rinse, de-seed and chop the bell peppers.

2 Trim the okras, cut off the stalk bit and make a wedge-shaped incision into their tips. Peel and finely chop the garlic. Rinse and pat dry the shrimps. Wash, scrub and drain the mussels. Rinse and trim the chillies, slice open, remove the seeds and finely chop the pods.

3 Heat the butter in a deep pan and gently fry the vegetables. Season with salt, pepper and chilli powder. Pour the stock and 500 ml/17 fl oz water over. Season to taste with Worcestershire sauce. Simmer over a low heat.

4 After approx. 10 minutes, add the seafood and leave to simmer for another 10 minutes.

Top and tail the okra pods.

■ Serves 4

2 onions

3 tomatoes

2 green bell peppers

300 g/10 oz okra pods

4 cloves garlic

500 g/17 oz peeled shrimps

500 g/17 oz mussels in their shell

2 chillies

4 tbsp butter

Salt, freshly ground pepper

1/2 tsp chilli powder

1 1/2 l/1 quart 13 fl oz chicken stock (cube)

2 tsp Worcestershire sauce

Preparation time: approx. 40 minutes

Nutrition information per serving approx.: 41 g P, 12 g F, 13 g C, 364 kcal/1530 kJ

TURKEY WITH SPICY BREAD STUFFING

■ Serves 4

1 turkey
(approx. 6 kg/13 lb)

2 cloves garlic

Salt, freshly ground pepper

5 onions

1 bunch parsley

800 g/1 lb 12 oz white bread

2 tbsp olive oil

100 g/3.5 oz bacon

300 g/10 oz chopped breakfast sausages

Chilli powder

4 tbsp butter

125 ml/4.5 fl oz dry white wine

1/4 l/9 fl oz vegetable stock (cube)

3 tbsp starch

100 g/3 fl oz double cream

Preparation time: approx. 4 hours

Nutrition information per serving approx.:
52 g P, 45 g F, 109 g C,
1154 kcal/4848 kJ

1 Trim the turkey, remove the bag of giblets, wash it from inside and outside, then pat it dry. Peel the garlic cloves, cut them in two and rub the turkey with the garlic. Season with salt and pepper.

2 Peel and chop the onions. Rinse and shake dry the parsley and mince it. Toast the white bread.

3 Heat the oil in a frying pan and gently fry the onions. Chop the bacon. Add the parsley, bacon and chopped breakfast sausage to the onions, season with salt, pepper and chilli powder. Preheat the oven to 180 °C/355 °F/gas mark 4.

4 Cut the toasted bread into cubes. Mix the onion-meat mix with the toast and knead well. Stuff the turkey with this mixture, pressing it with a small ladle. Tie the turkey up with kitchen string.

5 Heat the butter in a roasting pan and fry the turkey well on all sides. Then pour the wine and stock over it. Cook the turkey in the centre of the oven for approx. 3 hours. Every now and then, pour some of the stock over it.

6 Remove the turkey from the oven and keep warm. Fill the stock into a saucepan, bring to the boil and add starch and cream. Season the gravy with salt, pepper and chilli powder. Carve the turkey. Serve the turkey with the bread stuffing and gravy.

Rub the turkey with garlic.

Add toasted bread cubes to the mixture.

Fill the turkey.

Tie up the turkey.

Add the cream to the gravy.

BAKED POTATOES WITH CHEESE

Serves 4

8 medium large potatoes

3 tbsp oil

Salt

4 tbsp butter

Freshly ground pepper

2 red chillies

125 g/4.5 oz sour cream

2 egg yolks

Butter for the dish

100 g/3.5 oz grated Cheddar cheese

Preparation time: approx. 1 1/2 hours

Nutrition information per serving approx.: 12 g P, 32 g F, 31 g C, 490 kcal/2060 kJ

1 Preheat the oven to 200 °C/390 °F/ gas mark 6. Scrub the potatoes and brush with oil, then salt them. Lay the potatoes on a baking tray lined with greaseproof paper and bake them in the centre of the oven for approx. 1 hour.

2 Leave the potatoes to cool and cut a bit off the top of each one, like a lid. Carefully spoon out the potatoes with a teaspoon.

3 Mash the potato flesh with a fork, stir in the butter, season with salt and pepper.

4 Trim and rinse the chillies, de-seed and finely chop them. Mix the sour cream with the egg yolks, chillies and potato flesh and fill the potatoes with this mixture.

5 Brush an ovenproof dish with butter and place the potatoes in it, sprinkle with cheese and grill for approx. 5 minutes.

CLASSIC HAMBURGERS

1 Season the minced meat with salt and pepper. Form four meatballs. Heat the oil in a frying pan and fry the meatballs.

2 Trim and rinse the bell pepper, de-seed and cut into very fine slices.

3 Mix the bell pepper slices and coleslaw. Peel the onions and cut into rings. Rinse and trim the tomatoes and cut into slices.

4 Warm up the hamburger rolls in the oven. Rinse and dry the lettuce leaves, spread them over the lower parts of the rolls.

5 Spread the coleslaw salad over the lettuce leaves. Take the meatballs from the pan, pat them dry and place them on top of the coleslaw.

6 Now spread the onions and tomatoes over the meatballs and add a dash of ketchup and mayonnaise. Cover the hamburgers with the top half of the rolls and serve.

■ **Serves 4**

600 g/1 lb 5 oz minced meat

Salt

Freshly ground pepper

3 tbsp sunflower oil

1 green bell pepper

150 g/5 oz coleslaw

2 onions

2 tomatoes

4 hamburger rolls

A few lettuce leaves

3 tbsp ketchup

3 tbsp mayonnaise

Preparation time: approx. 20 minutes

Nutrition information per serving approx.: 26 g P, 25 g F, 12 g C, 396 kcal/1663 kJ

TRADITIONAL APPLE PIE

■ Serves 4

250 g/9 oz wheat flour

200 g/7 oz caster sugar

Salt

2 tbsp ground cinnamon

130 g/4.5 oz butter

3 tbsp oil

1/2 tsp vanilla essence

5 apples

1 tbsp lemon juice

250 g/9 oz quark

2 eggs

80 ml/2.5 fl oz milk

Butter for greasing the dish

1 egg yolk

Apricot jam

Preparation time: approx. 1 3/4 hours

Nutrition information per serving approx.: 19 g P, 43 g F, 121 g C, 990 kcal/4159 kJ

1 In a bowl, mix the flour with 1 tsp sugar, salt and 1 tbsp cinnamon. Knead the butter and oil into the pastry until it starts to get crumbly.

2 Add 5 tbsp water and the vanilla essence and knead into a smooth dough. Leave to rest in a cool place for approx. 1 hour.

3 Rinse and peel the apples and remove the pips and core. Cut the apples into rings and sprinkle with some lemon juice and then cover with the remaining sugar.

4 Mix the quark with the two eggs and the milk. Season to taste with cinnamon and sugar.

5 Preheat the oven to 230 °C/450 °F/ gas mark 8. Brush a pie dish of approx. 26 cm/10" Ø with butter.

6 Roll out one half of the dough on a work surface dusted with flour and place this into the bottom of the pie dish. Spread the quark mixture over the pastry dough and then cover with apple rings.

7 Roll out the remaining pastry, cut into strips and lay across the apples, patterned like a grille. Beat the egg yolk and brush the pie with it.

8 Bake the apple pie in the centre of the oven for approx. 15 minutes. Then turn the oven down to 180 °C/355 °F/gas mark 4 and bake for another 45 minutes. Heat a little apricot jam in a pan and glaze the cake with it once it has cooled.

APPLES

For this apple pie, varieties that go soft during the baking process are suited best. One very flavourful variety is Cox.

ORIGINAL AMERICAN DOUGHNUTS

SUGGESTED DRINK

Doughnuts go well with a sweet coffee drink: per serving, mix 40 ml/1.5 fl oz coffee liqueur with 30 ml/ 1 fl oz whiskey and 40 ml/1.5 fl oz cream and serve in a cocktail glass.

■ **Serves 4**

50 g/1.75 oz soft butter

3 eggs

150 g/5 oz caster sugar

200 ml/7 oz milk

1 tbsp custard powder

Salt

Freshly ground nutmeg

650 g/1 lb 7 oz flour

1 pack baking powder

Oil for the deep fat fryer

Sugar for dipping

Preparation time: approx. 30 minutes

Nutrition information per serving approx.: 24 g P, 20 g F, 144 g C, 896 kcal/3764 kJ

1 Whisk the butter with eggs and sugar until it gets foamy. Stir in milk, custard powder, salt and nutmeg.

2 Mix the flour with the baking powder and slowly add to the dough.

3 Dust your work surface with flour, then roll out the dough, leaving it approx. 1 cm/0.4" thick. Cut out the dough with a doughnut cutter. If you should not have one, take a round cutter of approx. 7 cm/3" Ø.

4 Now cut small holes out of the centre to make rings.

5 Heat the oil in a deep fat fryer and fry the doughnuts until they are golden brown. Let them drip off and then dip both sides in the sugar. Serve immediately.

CHOCOLATE BROWNIES

1 Melt the chocolate and butter in a *bain-marie* over a low heat and stir. Preheat the oven to 180 °C/355 °F/gas mark 4.

2 Take the saucepan from the heat and stir in the sugar. Leave to cool.

3 Beat the eggs, vanilla essence and chocolate cream.

4 Stir in the flour, baking powder and salt and quickly work into a smooth dough.

5 Stir in the chopped walnuts. Spread the dough on a baking tray lined with greaseproof paper and bake in the centre of the oven for approx. 50 minutes.

6 Remove from the oven, leave to cool and cut into squares. Serve the brownies on a tray or large plate.

Cut the cake into squares.

■ **Serves 4**

200 g/7 oz dark chocolate

125 g/4.5 oz butter

200 g/7 oz caster sugar

2 eggs

1 tsp vanilla essence

200 g/7 oz flour

1 tsp baking powder

1/4 tsp salt

150 g/5 oz chopped walnuts

Preparation time: approx. 1 1/4 hours

Nutrition information per serving approx.: 7 g P, 6 g F, 61 g C, 347 kcal/1460 kJ

PARTY RECIPES

The dishes characteristic for Tex-Mex cooking are ideal for parties and barbecues. This chapter offers two unusual alternatives including recipes, drinks and table decorations.

FILLED PEPPERS

DISH OF SNACKS

SUGGESTED DRINK

As a drink to go with these dishes, we recommend a Rosebud. Per person, blend 50 g/1.75 oz raspberries with 4 tbsp tequila and 2 tsp caster sugar. Mix with 125 ml/4.5 fl oz orange juice and serve with crushed ice.

■ Serves 8

24 red peppers

1 kg/2 lb 3 oz mixed minced meat

Salt

Freshly ground pepper

Chilli powder

200 g/7 oz full fat cream cheese

4 tbsp garlic oil

Preparation time: approx. 45 minutes

Nutrition information per serving approx.: 28 g P, 35 g F, 5 g C, 490 kcal/2059 kJ

1 Trim and rinse the peppers and cut off the top third, length-wise.

2 Mix the minced meat with spices and cream cheese and fill into the pepper pods.

3 Brush with garlic oil and grill for approx. 18 minutes.

■ Serves 8

300 g/10 oz minced beef

100 g/3.5 oz cooked rice

1 egg, garlic salt

Freshly ground pepper

Chilli powder

3 tbsp butter

200 g/7 oz Spanish salami

200 g/7 oz black olives

250 g/9 oz pickled red and green peppers

3 avocados

1 chopped chilli

3 tbsp crème fraîche

Lemon juice

200 g/7 oz nacho chips

100 g/3.5 oz tortilla chips

Preparation time: approx. 45 minutes

Nutrition information per serving approx.: 29 g P, 52 g F, 13 g C, 679 kcal/2851 kJ

1 Mix the minced meat with the rice, egg and spices. Form small balls. Heat the butter in a frying pan and fry the meatballs. Cut the salami into thin slices. Drain the olives and peppers.

2 Peel the avocados, remove the stone and mix the flesh with the chopped chilli, crème fraîche and lemon juice. Season to taste with the spices. Arrange all the ingredients and the avocado dip on a large plate and serve with nachos and tortilla chips.

MEXICAN FIESTA

■ *Bright colours such as blue, red and green will give your fiesta the appropriate Mexican flair. A good idea is to serve the dishes in earthenware pots or plates. A chain made of dried chillies is another charming idea for decoration. Napkins with Mexican decor can be created without much fuss, but they can also be bought in large household stores. Pieces of flower pots painted with bright colours are another colourful item for decorating your tables with.*

SPARERIBS

SUGGESTED DRINK

Our recommended drink is a
Bloody Mary. Per portion, mix
1/4 tsp Worcestershire sauce
with 1/4 tbsp lemon juice,
50 ml/2 fl oz gin and
75 ml/2.5 fl oz tomato
juice. Season to taste
with salt and pepper.

TEXAN BARBECUE

■ **Serves 8**

2 kg/4 lb 6 oz
pork ribs

3 l/3 quarts
vegetable stock

1 bay leaf

2 clovers

1 tbsp chopped onions

300 ml/10 fl oz
ketchup

5 tbsp brown sugar

5 tbsp wine vinegar

5 tbsp Worcestershire
sauce

1/2 tsp mustard
powder

A few dashes
Tabasco sauce

Salt

Freshly ground pepper

Preparation time:
approx. 1 hour

Time for marinating:
approx. 10 hours

Nutrition information
per serving approx.:
89 g P, 65 g F, 2 g C,
958 kcal/4023 kJ

1 Separate the ribs. Mix the stock with
the spices and boil the meat in this
stock until it starts to slightly come off the
bone. In the meantime, mix the onion and
ketchup with the other ingredients in a
bowl. Marinate the meat in this paste for
approx. 10 hours.

2 Remove the meat, pat dry, and cook on
the grill for approx. 30 minutes. Brush
with the sauce regularly. Heat up the sauce,
season with salt and pepper and serve with
the spareribs.

GRILLED CORN ON THE COB

1 Trim and rinse the corn cobs and season with salt, pepper and chilli powder.

2 Spread the butter over the cobs and wrap them in tin foil. Cook in the grill or embers for approx. 10 minutes. Corn on the cob is delicious with a yoghurt dip.

■ Serves 8

8 corn cobs

Salt, freshly ground pepper

Chilli powder

100 g/3.5 oz butter

Preparation time: approx. 20 minutes

Nutrition information per serving approx.: 6 g P, 23 g F, 43 g C, 426 kcal/1792 kJ

CHEF'S SALAD

1 Rinse and dry the lettuce and pluck into mouth-size pieces. Cut the turkey breast into small strips. Cut the cheese into small cubes. Peel the onions and cut them into rings.

2 Rinse the tomatoes and cut into slices. Peel the eggs and slice them, too. Mix all the salad ingredients in a bowl and serve garnished with Thousand Islands dressing.

■ Serves 8

1 iceberg lettuce

150 g/5 oz roast turkey breast

200 g/7 oz Swiss cheese

2 onions

4 tomatoes

4 hard-boiled eggs

150 ml/5 oz Thousand Islands salad dressing

Preparation time: approx. 30 minutes

Nutrition information per serving approx.: 33 g P, 12 g F, 4 g C, 371 kcal/1558 kJ

■ *Texan cooking also goes well served in rustic earthenware or terracotta-style pottery.*

Arrange the cutlery and dishes on a large block of wood or on a rustic wooden table. White sand or pebbles make for ideal decoration instead of a table cloth. Do you own any cactuses? Place them in the sand and cover the plant pots or roots with sand – hey presto, here's a desert landscape.

An old coach wheel or pole, a horse's halter or a sombrero, cowboy's hat or spurs further evoke a taste of the Wild West.